Jane Butel's TEX-MEX COOKBOOK

Jane Butel's TEX-MEX COOKBOOK

BY JANE BUTEL
Designed by Milton Glaser, Inc.

HARMONY BOOKS
New York

Inquiries should be addressed to:
Harmony Books
a division of Crown Publishers, Inc.
One Park Avenue, New York, New York 10016

Published simultaneously in Canada by General
Publishing Co., Ltd. Printed in the United States of
America.

Library of Congress Cataloging in Publication Data

Butel, Jane.
    Jane Butel's Tex-Mex cookbook.

    1. Cookery, American—Southwestern States.
I. Title.   II. Title: Tex-Mex cookbook.
TX715.B984   1980   641.5′979   79-25017
ISBN 0-517-539861

To my daughter, Amy

CONTENTS

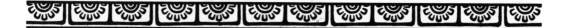

ACKNOWLEDGMENTS

I wish to thank all those who have worked with great dedication to make this book a reality.

For over ten years, close friends in New Mexico, such as Lyn Ortega, Mary Salzer-Nobles, Jenny Candelaria and Janet Pugh, helped supply ideas, test recipes and develop practical hints.

Lark L. Wittens, Milton Glaser, Santiago Moneo, Ben Roth and a host of very close and dear associates have been a constant source of help and inspiration.

INTRODUCTION

As far back as memory takes me, I remember the spicy simmering stews and sauces my family called Mexican food. Usually, it was chile con carne, or chile, as we all called it. I ate it in a wide range of forms and temperaments, with a sauce so fiery hot it could barely be eaten to a much milder stew concoction. For years those dishes were my only conception of Mexican foods, until I learned from my Mexican aunt that "our" chile con carne, or chile, wasn't even Mexican!

Perhaps you, too, thought that the reddish bean stew was the national dish of Mexico. Not so! The state of Texas has been credited with creating the dish we know as chile. Yet in the Southwest area of the United States, Texas included, chile sauces can be made from green or red chiles, with or without meat or beans. Chile then is not necessarily chile con carne, but a thick stew or sauce flavored with chile.

Many other dishes that you might have thought of as Mexican are really from the border states of Texas, New Mexico and Arizona. In that region Tex-Mex is the label most used for what we all think of as "Mexican food," which is quite different from Old Mexico cooking.

So much of America has grown to like this spicy, colorful food that thousands of taco stands, chile parlors and prepared mixtures abound. But because of bulk preparation, shortcuts, the lack of fresh pure seasonings and the deletion of the traditional techniques for combining ingredients, the true flavors are lost. This convenient fare is a poor substitute for the delectable subtleties and outstanding flavors, color and genuine great eating possible with authentic Tex-Mex foods. I want to share with you the good taste treats so lacking in today's popular Mexican foods.

The origin of Tex-Mex cooking is definitely Mexican: it was the early Indian cultures of the Mayans and Aztecs who introduced tomatoes, avocados, peanuts, squash, sweet and white potatoes, pineapple, papayas, vanilla, cocoa, a few kinds of beans and chile peppers to the conquering Spanish. The Spaniards immediately took a liking to many of the new and different delicacies in Mexico and carried them back to Spain where they quickly spread to the rest of the world.

On the other hand, the Spanish introduced cattle, sheep, chickens, wheat, rice, nuts, wines, oils, cloves, cinnamon and other spices and fruits to the Mayans and Aztecs. The missionary nuns of Mexico were responsible for developing many new foods, using the combined influences and products of the Indians and Spanish. One such dish attributed to these ladies is mole poblano, which they created to celebrate a special occasion by blending together most all the ingredients they had on hand. Mole is the spiced chocolate sauce laden with fruits, nuts and chiles, served over chicken.

As Mexican cookery gained popularity in the United States border states, American Indians and frontier cooks adapted the food to suit their tastes and available local ingredients. New foods such as corn, squash, melons and pumpkins were added to the food preparations along with many indigenous American ingredients. Beyond Texas borders, the chile that is considered to be truly native to New Mexico is a red or green chile pepper sauce with finely cubed or shredded meat served atop stewed pinto beans. The meat and beans are never mixed.

Because of adaptations such as chile con carne and frito pie, Texas, perhaps more than the other border states, seems best described as the source of simplicity. They often cut back on ingredients and make their cooking as easy as possible, whereas the cuisine has been innovatively developed in Arizona and California. These last two states use fruits, vegetables, sour cream and olives in greater abundance and tend to combine more foods creatively than in other Mexican border states: some examples are stuffed avocados, sour cream on enchiladas and chile, original salads piled high on tostados and unrecognizably elegant chimichangos and flautas. New Mexico, however, has retained more authentic dishes and traditional methods. It is more purely Mexican- and Indian-influenced than the other border states. The New Mexican natives have a 350-year-old tradition of adapting Old Mexican foods to their liking. They are known to use more chile and cook more foods from "scratch." The foods are simple and traditional, often requiring specialized cooking techniques. Navajo bread, sopaipillas, and Indian bear claw bread are typical examples. The distances and years have given rise to many variations, creating a great regional Tex-Mex cuisine.

Many myths abound about Mexican foods. Other than the geographic confusion about what Mexican food really is, most people think that anything Mexican must be fiery hot. Nothing could be further from the truth. In fact, many favorite dishes are not hot at all. In my opinion, the best way to enjoy Tex-Mex is to balance spiciness with color and texture. I always serve a hot chile-laden main dish like tamales with a mild side dish of posole and a crisp cool vegetable salad or creamy heap of guacamole.

With great pleasure I share with you my collection of favorite recipes and cooking secrets. Passed on by native Indian, Mexican and Spanish

cooks in the Southwestern states, many are generations, even centuries, old. Each recipe has been carefully tested and painstakingly developed from handfuls, bagfuls and "mix-until-it-looks-right" instructions. Some of the complementary dishes, such as the avocado and grapefruit salad with poppy-seed dressing, taste delicious with the traditional foods.

To these wonderful Southwestern cooks, my aunt and dear staff who worked with me for ten years, I owe my heartfelt thanks; I'm sure you will add yours.

The purpose of this book is to share the very best-tested recipes I could find and develop for favorite Mexican foods. Tips for garnishing and freezing, menus, and time-saving methods of preparation are included to help you create meals with Mexican gusto—Tex-Mex style!

Buen apetito!

Jane Butel

INGREDIENTS & EQUIPMENT

Most people haven't had the opportunity to taste how great Tex-Mex food can be. While I was Home Service Director for Public Service Company of New Mexico, I was able to develop many failproof recipes for Southwest specialty foods that require special techniques. My staff of home economists and kitchen helpers, as well as many who attended our cooking classes, graciously shared their favorite recipes and tips for such secrets as how to make hollow and fluffy sopaipillas, perfectly shaped tamales, beautifully scalloped empanadas or round chiles rellenos.

The enthusiasm for learning more and more about cooking these foods led visitors and newcomers to write thousands of letters and call continuously asking how they could make those delicious, attractive dishes. One woman from Cleveland, Ohio, simply wouldn't give up. Following a vacation, she started a letter-writing campaign to various editors and restaurateurs in her home state, but unfortunately, they could not fill her requests. Finally, though, her search for a recipe for sopaipillas came to my attention and I sent her the recipe. She was so impressed she contacted the food editor of the *Cleveland Plain Dealer* who ran a full-page story on her, me, the recipe and the many, many persistent letters she had written.

Cooking and eating are very personal pleasures, and recipes are merely a guide to use to develop your own favorite foods. With this in mind, remember that your taste preference may from time to time dictate variations in the character or pungency of the ingredients. To be sure you develop the flavor *you* like each time, follow the basic instructions of the recipe and taste the food as it is cooking, altering the seasoning to please your own tastebuds.

Always keep in mind that chile, the mainstay ingredient for Tex-Mex food, as with salt or any other strong flavoring, should be used first in moderation—you can always add more, but once added it's impossible to remove. A good rule to follow, especially when serving guests who are new to Tex-Mex cooking, is to prepare the dish using mild seasonings, particularly a mild chile. Then serve a side dish of hot, spicy salsa, or sauce, for those who like it hotter.

Tex-Mex foods have much to recommend them, they are fun and easy to prepare, very hearty and relatively low in cost. Since only a few basic ingredients are used, try to seek out fresh, pure, top-quality authentic ingredients. Substitutions can change the flavor and even the texture and color. Most of the basic ingredients are easily obtained. The more unusual ones are available through Mail Order Sources (p. 181).

For beef, lean prime or choice chopped steak will make a more savory stew or main dish than will ordinary lesser cuts of ground beef. This applies critically to the seasonings that create the authentic flavor; substitutions can completely change the personality of a food. Take the time to stew the sauces, to carefully chop the ingredients and to serve the foods attractively garnished. If possible, serve them on rustic Mexican pottery and bright-colored tablecloths or placemats, for a next-to-the-border feeling.

For your convenience, I have written the instructions for use with popular cooking equipment and electric appliances such as the blender, food processor, deep-fryer, mixer and freezer. Many Tex-Mex dishes can be prepared in a microwave oven. I use mine for melting cheese, warming casseroles and sautéing.

The following is a list of optional equipment that can be used to prepare Tex-Mex specialties. However, you can prepare any recipe without them. If you would like to order any of the items below check the Mail Order Sources on page 181.

Tortilla press: If you would like to make your own tortillas you will probably want to invest in one, as it takes a lot of practice to flip-flop them, as experienced regional cooks do, to get them as thin as you want.

Metate: This is the Mexican or Southwestern version of a mortar and pestle. A blender or a food processor will do the job.

Bollito: This is a special, thin, round rolling pin perfect for flour tortillas. The easiest way to get your own bollito is to go to any wood-working shop and ask for an 8-inch length of 2-inch doweling.

Black cast-iron tapa: Usually Southwesterners use a cast-iron, well-seasoned wood- or coal-burning stove lid insert. A cast-iron griddle works about as well. The dark surface is preferable for the final appearance, as it provides a hotter surface that gives tortillas the dark brown speckles.

Molinillo: This gadget really has no substitute. It is used for whipping hot chocolate. You roll the round handle between your palms and the cut-out circles whip the chocolate as it cooks.

Mexican dishes freeze exceptionally well, especially the stews, sauces and masa foods such as tamales, all keeping the flavor you intended. Recent research at New Mexico State University has shown that the spice chile works as an added preservative, actually prolonging the "keeping quality" of meats.

CHILE

Chile, the seasoning, not the soup or stew, is the key to Mexican food, unlocking the cuisine's unique flavors. Generally every Tex-Mex meal has at least one dish with some form of chile seasoning. The wide range of chiles—from hot to mild, red to green, small to large, and fresh to dried—allows you to be creative.

Chile is mysteriously complex. It not only determines the mildness or hotness of Mexican food but the more subtle and far more elusive elements of "flavor." The range of flavors possible is due to the number of varieties of chile. There are over twenty different types, each contributing a different flavor influenced by the growing conditions and climate. Chile easily cross-pollinates, producing more than one type and piquancy on a single plant. (Warm, long growing days produce the mildest chiles.) If by chance, the chile you are using is hotter than you like, you can "tame" it by adding tomato sauce or juice. A word of caution—adding tomato is considered a Gringo or newcomer trait which true aficionados such as myself disparage.

Chile is usually spelled several ways, but I always use the Southwestern or Mexican *chile* spelling. Many American cookbooks and spice companies use *chili*, while the British often use *chilli* for the spice and the stew. Chiles or chile peppers are not related to the spice pepper, which produces black and white pepper. The word *pepper* is a misnomer. Chiles are *Capsicum frutescens*, the same general family, Solanaceae, as potatoes, tomatoes and eggplants. Hotness ranges from none at all, as in the bell pepper, to the pequín, which I think is close to fire.

A New Mexico legend about chile holds that "it protects against colds and malaria, it aids digestion, it clarifies the blood, it develops robustness and resistance to the elements; it even acts as a stimulant to the romantically inclined." I can't vouch for any health cures, but its inclusion in your cooking will delight you and your guests, therefore certainly adding to everyone's pleasure.

Chile has an outstanding sweet flavor, but if not well stored, will begin losing its flavor. To prevent this oxidation, ground chile must be stored in an airtight dark container and placed in a cool place to prevent sun, heat or light from destroying the flavor.

The ground chile specified in this book is pure ground chile, not the blended spice, so-called chili powder, that is dark brownish in color and is sold in the spice section of supermarkets. The dark brownish mixture possesses quite a different flavor, resulting initially from the chiles used and the oxidation of flavors, but also it has been mixed with garlic powder, orégano and comino, which alters the taste significantly.

The deep-red, ground pure chile produces much fresher, sweeter and full-bodied flavors in foods. Always try to buy the reddest, freshest and best-packaged chile available. Foil or other nonoxidizing packaging preserves the fresh flavor.

The mildest chile results from using a mild type of chile that has been ground without seeds and ribs. Always remember that seeds and ribs carry the heat in chile; removing them makes any chile milder. However, in ground chile it is often hard to tell whether it is ground without them. Using chile caribe or grinding chiles yourself is the best way to be sure seeds and ribs are discarded.

The two most popular types for use as green chiles or for dried red chile powder are the hybrids developed in California and New Mexico. Generally, these chiles are long, wide shouldered at the stem end, with blunt tips and waxy skins. Most other chiles are smaller and either roundish or very skinny. Other types in American markets are the ancho, jalapeño, serrano or pequín chiles. There are recognizable differences.

Ancho chiles (ahn-cho): These look similar to the bell pepper but are considerably more peppery: they have a firm texture, a bit darker green color when fresh, a shinier skin and more tapered general conformation. When dried, they become dark red, almost black. They are difficult to obtain, so none of the recipes in this book specify ancho chiles.

Jalapeño chiles (hall-la-páy-nyoh): When fresh these chiles have a dark-green, round, firm appearance and are about 2½ inches long and about 1 inch across. They are extremely hot. Canned or bottled jalapeños are generally available in most supermarkets.

Serrano chiles (seh-rrráh-no): These tiny, thin peppers are a deep waxy green, 1 to 1½ inches long, about ½ inch thick and are very, very hot. They are rarely available fresh; usually available pickled.

Pequín chiles (peh-keén): These small, oval chiles usually sold dried, often crushed, are referred to as *quebrado*. They are very hot.

CHILE CARIBE

Caribe is a more subtly flavored chile and can be substituted for chile powder. Most native Southwesterners prefer it, especially for enchiladas. Caribe chile requires an additional step to prepare. The caribe is made from chiles that have been tied into a *ristra*, or string, dried in the sun and usually hung in the kitchen for convenience as well as decoration. When you want to use some caribe just pluck them from your *ristra*. Rinse them, remove the stem, shake out the seeds, crush, roast, simmer and strain. Chile caribe is also available commercially, ready for roasting.

Pure chile powder is made by grinding dried chiles including peel, and sometimes ribs and seeds, to produce a stronger flavor. To substitute caribe in a recipe calling for chile powder, remember that 1 cup of pulp made as below equals 6 tablespoons of chile powder and 1 tablespoon flour.

To Prepare Caribe

Place the crushed chiles in a large shallow pan and roast them in a 300°F. oven for 15 minutes, or until the color darkens. For every cup of roasted chiles, add 4 cups water and simmer for 30 minutes. Strain through a fine sieve. Substitute this liquid for the liquid and chile powder in any chile recipe.

Caribe can be frozen in ice-cube trays; when solidly frozen, store cubes in plastic freezer bags.

GREEN CHILE

The best-flavored green chile is preferably fresh, but frozen will do. Canned chiles are a poor substitute, especially for dishes where green chile is a major ingredient, such as chiles rellenos, chile pie or omelets.

Increasingly, the New Mexico or California type of chiles are available in markets throughout the United States. If they are not, a milder substitute is the Italian or frying pepper. Select chiles that are shiny and free from blemishes. They should not be picked until the dark-green color lightens somewhat just before turning red. However, there is quite a range of shades of green, depending upon the variety. Usually the lighter the green and the blunter the tip, the milder the chile will be. The darkest green ones with narrow pointed tips are usually quite hot. The mildest chiles are raised in southern, warm climates where they mature rapidly. Chiles need sandy soil and lots of moisture, making river valleys of the Southwestern states perfect growing places.

The tough outer skin of green chiles must be removed before they can be used. Parching chiles is quite easy and is the best way to remove the skin. Be sure to follow all the steps closely for easy peeling.

To Parch Green Chiles

1 Rinse the chiles and drain. Pierce each chile close to the stem, using a sharp pointed knife, toothpick or ice pick. If chile is large, pierce twice, once on either side.

2 Place chiles on a cookie sheet covered with foil and place under a broiler. If using an electric range, place rack so tops of chiles are 4 to 6 inches from broiler unit; if using a gas range, place broiler rack in top position closest to the flame; if using charcoal, do not use foil and place rack about 5 inches above the heat. Rotate chiles as they turn amber and the skin develops blisters. Blister uniformly.

3 Remove chiles from cookie sheet and place in a bowl or clean sink and cover with a cold, damp towel for 10 minutes. This steams the chiles and makes peeling much easier. If you want the chiles to be crisp, place cracked ice on the hot chiles instead of covering with a towel. Never place in ice water, though, as they will become soggy.

4 Starting at the stem end, peel the outer skin downward. If using them for chiles rellenos, leave the stems on; otherwise, remove. Remove the seeds and ribs after taking off the stem. Use chiles as desired.

To Freeze: *Chiles can be frozen either before or after peeling. I usually freeze them unpeeled because they peel much easier after freezing, and they retain their shape better.*

Maximum Recommended Freezer Storage: *12 months*

SPICES & SEASONINGS

Early Southwestern settlers used very few spices, only those available on the hillsides and slopes. To this day, this influence pervades. In addition to chile the basic flavorings for meat and vegetable dishes are onions, salt, garlic and orégano. Comino (cumin) is almost as popular, although not considered as necessary due to its scarcity in earlier times. Anise, coriander (cilantro) and, occasionally, wild mint are used to flavor desserts.

Following is a list of spices and seasonings most often used in Tex-Mex cooking:

Anise: A licorice-flavored spice found on the hillsides. The seeds are dried and stored. Many baked products such as cookies include aniseed.

Azafran (wild saffron): Different from imported saffron, the wild variety almost completely lacks flavor and is used for color.

Comino (cumin): The seeds of this wild plant are dried and usually crushed for use in red chile dishes and stews.

Cilantro (coriander): The leaves are generally called cilantro and are used in vegetable, chile and fish dishes. Fresh cilantro, though it adds a unique flavor, cannot be satisfactorily dried or frozen and in my opinion should be left out rather than substituting any form of preserved cilantro or the mature coriander seed. Chinese parsley is the same thing and in many areas an Oriental market is the best place to buy fresh cilantro.

Garlic: A popular seasoning very compatible with chile and Mexican food flavors; whole garlic should always be used. Garlic powder or juice just don't give the same flavor.

Laurel (bay leaves): Bay leaves are popular in meat and vegetable dishes. The Spanish taught the early settlers how to grow the plants and dry the leaves.

Orégano: The Southwestern, Mexican-type orégano grows abundantly throughout the Southwest and is a different variety from the Greek or Italian herb. As with anise, orégano was used generously in many meat or chile dishes. Cooks almost always added a pinch to the pot. Many Mexicans, particularly the Indians, still gather the leaves of the plant, dry them and use them by crushing the leaves between their palms to add to foods.

Sage: Varying with families and depending upon the altitude, sage is sometimes used in meat dishes. It is deeply colored and often called black sage. This grows wild at high altitudes. The leaves are dried and crushed for use like oregano.

Yerba buena (wild mint): Fresh or dried mint is used to flavor many foods. Some even put a pinch of dried mint in meat and vegetable dishes.

SHORTENING

Some people cringe when they learn that lard or bacon drippings are the usual shortening for most Tex-Mex cooking. When making tortillas, tamales or delicate pastries, lard is the favorite. Deep-frying is generally also done in lard. More recent generations are now occasionally using margarine or cooking oil. Butter does not work well. For flavoring vegetables, meats and stews, bacon drippings are used. For any dietary or preference reason, substitute a no-cholesterol type margarine or a hydrogenated shortening for lard in the recipes. Use butter or margarine in place of bacon drippings, and oil when frying.

CHEESE

The most popular cheese overall is Monterey Jack, which is a California product developed in the town of Monterey decades ago. It is sold nationwide. It is a semisoft cheese not unlike Munster in texture. Because of its sharpish, yet mild flavor and superior melting qualities, it is my choice for most Mexican recipes and I usually designate it. However, if you have trouble locating Monterey Jack, you may successfully substitute Longhorn Cheddar, as it is the closest in flavor and quality. Don't use processed American cheese or Parmesan as a substitute, either will drastically alter the flavor of Tex-Mex dishes.

SOUR CREAM

A relatively recent favorite topper to most any Tex-Mex specialty is sour cream. Originally used in California and Arizona, it is now popular throughout the area and is served either plain or mixed with lime juice, onion, cheese or all three. Enchiladas, tacos, burritos, and flautas are delicious served with sour cream.

MASA

Dried corn ground into masa is the basis for breads and many dishes such as tortillas and tamales. You can purchase the regular dried masa in most every city now. If you have trouble finding it, you can order it from the Mail Order Sources (p. 181). Those lucky enough to live near a tortilla factory should buy the prepared masa for a fresher flavor and convenience.

Lucky New Mexicans can also buy the traditional blue cornmeal masa. Increasingly it is being packaged for out-of-state sales, so perhaps you can buy or mail order it. The flavor is extraordinary as the corn is roasted before milling. Also, I believe this variety of corn, which is deep blue in color, seems to possess a much fuller flavor—richer and more nutlike.

BEANS

The bean generally used is the pinto bean, a medium-size, longish bean that is speckled brown if it is good and freshly dried. When stewed, pintos turn a light pinkish color. There really is no substitute, as any other bean substantially changes the flavor of the dish. Since I've never had trouble buying these, canned or dried, I believe you won't either. Of course they can be ordered. By the way, the freshly cooked or home-frozen beans are far superior to the canned variety.

AVOCADOS

In the Southwest top-quality avocados for making guacamole and Mexican soups and dishes are available year round. The best are either the black, nobby-skinned Has variety or the small, black, speckled, light-green, thin-skinned Fuertes ones, both California or Mexico grown. The jumbo-size bright-green variety is generally less than ideal for Mexican dishes as it is more watery textured, sweeter and gives a flavor that is less desirable. Never wait until the day you wish to serve avocados to shop for them because you will generally be out of luck—particularly out in the Southwest. A ripe avocado should be soft when pressed, and the seed should shake. When peeled, the skin should stick, yet easily yield to spoon or knife. A rich buttery flesh should be easily scooped out. Yes, scooped, unless you wish to have perfect slices. The fastest and easiest way to get the meat from an avocado is not to peel it at all, but to cut it into halves and scoop out the flesh with a spoon.

There are many myths about speeding ripening. I haven't found that sticking them in a plastic bag in flour or other meal speeds up the process. Sitting them in the bright sun can cause sunburned spots in the flesh. The best method is to plan ahead at least 3 days or so and let them ripen on a shelf in the kitchen away from bright sunlight. Refrigerate them as soon as the flesh is soft when pressed.

CHORIZO

This spicy pork and beef Spanish-type sausage is excellent in many dishes and really has no substitute. The hotness varies. Usually chorizo is sold in chubby links which are available throughout the Southwest; elsewhere they can be found in Mexican or Spanish specialty markets. To use, you usually remove the casing and crumble the sausage before cooking. You may mix in some cooked ground beef if you have purchased chorizo that's too hot. Perhaps you will want to try your own hand at making some as it is not particularly hard to do, especially if you own a food processor, just a bit messy. If you are having trouble buying them, I think making them in batches for the freezer is the best bet. See recipe, p. 130.

APPETIZERS

Tex-Mex appetizers and snacks are more special than those served in any other region in our country. They always seem to impart a party or fiesta feeling. Chiles, garlic, onions, tomatoes and cheeses combine in many tasty combinations to temper the palate for the main-dish foods.

The two best-known appetizers are guacamole and chile con queso, both traditionally served with tostados. Once you savor the goodness of homemade tostados prepared from deep-fried fresh corn tortillas, you will find commercially prepared varieties a poor substitute. Never serve potato chips! For those watching their waistlines you can substitute fresh vegetables in place of tostados.

Nachos can be served simply with refried beans topped with chile and cheese atop a tostado, or with toppings such as sour cream and olives.

Chile or chick-pea nuts and tiny snack-size empanadas are more unusual but great to have on hand for snacking; they are easily kept frozen. Whichever combination of goodies you select for serving I'm sure you'll get to know what I mean about the mood they set, especially when you complement them with Margaritas or Mexican beer.

GUACAMOLE
Avocado Dip

2 cups

Guacamole is the traditional Southwestern dip, often served with crisp tostados or fresh vegetables. Of all the recipes I have tasted, this one outshines them all.

2 avocados
2 teaspoons fresh lime juice
½ teaspoon salt
2 green onions
½ fresh tomato, peeled and finely chopped
1 garlic clove, crushed
2 tablespoons finely chopped green chile, or 1 small pickled jalapeño, finely chopped
½ teaspoon minced fresh cilantro (optional)

1 Cut the avocados into halves, remove the pits, and scoop the flesh into a mixing bowl.

2 Mash with a fork or masher, then add the lime juice and salt and mix well.

3 Stir in remaining ingredients and mix until all are evenly distributed.

4 Taste and adjust seasoning. Some like guacamole hot while others like it quite mild. Often the piquancy is best determined by the other foods you are serving. If some like it hot and others don't, a solution is to serve a side dish of spicy Salsa (p. 42).

5 Serve guacamole in a Mexican pottery bowl and garnish the top with a few tostados thrust into top. Serve with a basket of tostados. As a salad, serve over chopped lettuce and garnish each serving with a cherry tomato.

Variation: *A less traditional method for preparing guacamole is to mix all the ingredients together in a blender or food processor. The compromise is that the pulverizing not only alters the authentic texture, but it seems to create a somewhat harsher flavor.*

Note: *Many myths seem to abound about placing an avocado pit in the guacamole to keep it from discoloring or oxidizing. I don't find that to work so well. Cover the guacamole well or sprinkle with a few drops of ascorbic-acid mixture, the mixture used to prevent darkening in freezing fruits. Be careful when adding the acid not to add too much as it can slightly sweeten the flavor of the guacamole.*

CHILE CON QUESO
Chile Cheese Dip

1¾ cups

This dip is no longer unique to the Southwest as it once was. Tostados are far and away the best dippers.

1 cup Monterey Jack cheese
½ cup Cheddar cheese
¼ cup heavy cream
1 medium-size fresh tomato, peeled and finely chopped
1 medium-size sweet onion, finely chopped
¼ cup chopped parched green chiles (p. 21)
1 garlic clove, crushed

1 Melt both cheeses together in a heavy saucepan or double boiler over low heat.

2 After cheese melts, add cream, stirring constantly.

3 Add chopped tomato, onion, green chile and garlic. Stir to blend all flavors. More cream may be needed; if so, add only a few drops at a time.

4 Serve warm in a chafing dish or a dish set over a candle warmer. Serve with tostados.

Note: *If ever there's any leftover dip, save it for instant nachos made by scooping the chili con queso onto tostados and heating. Chile con queso makes an excellent sauce or filler for omelets, enchiladas and hamburgers.*

Maximum Recommended Freezer Storage: *4 months*

GREEN CHILE DIP

2 cups

This dip is a favorite standby throughout the Southwest. Serve with tostados.

2 cups sour cream
1 garlic clove, minced
2 to 4 green chiles, chopped
dash of salt

1 Combine all ingredients, adjusting the amount of chiles to your taste. Chill for at least 1 hour before serving.

Variation: *Save calories by substituting yogurt or blended cottage cheese for the sour cream.*

Not Recommended for Freezing

HOT MASHED BEAN DIP

2 cups

This hearty dip's milder flavor contrasts nicely with spicier ones.

2 cups drained, cooked Pinto Beans (p. 153)
2 scallions, minced
¾ cup grated Monterey Jack or Cheddar cheese
¼ teaspoon minced cilantro
1 tablespoon ground mild red chile
½ teaspoon salt
1 garlic clove, crushed
2 tablespoons bacon fat, lard or butter

1 Mash the beans, add the other ingredients except the fat, and mix well, seasoning with salt and garlic to taste.

2 Heat the fat in a chafing dish, add the mixture, and stir until the cheese is melted and the dip is bubbling. Serve warm with freshly made tostados.

Note: *Leftover dip can be refrozen and used as a filling for burritos or tacos or as a layer on nachos.*

Maximum Recommended Freezer Storage: *3 months*

GARBANZO NUTS
Deep-Fried Chick-Peas

2½ cups

An excellent crunchy snack to have on tap for light snacking and parties. If a freezer is handy, for your own convenience, double or triple the recipe.

1 pound dried chick-peas
¼ pound butter
4 garlic cloves, crushed
½ teaspoon dry mustard
1 teaspoon ground mild red chile
¼ teaspoon crushed coriander seed
2 teaspoons salt
1 teaspoon onion salt
1 teaspoon ground ginger
½ teaspoon garlic salt
3 teaspoons soy sauce

1 Soak the chick-peas in water to cover overnight. Drain. Cook in well-salted water until they are nearly done but still a bit hard, about 1 hour. Drain.

2 Divide cooked chick-peas into 2 portions. Melt 4 tablespoons butter in each of 2 skillets, then sauté 2 crushed garlic cloves in each.

3 Remove garlic. Add half of the chick-peas to each skillet and sauté very slowly, stirring often until they begin to sizzle and turn golden brown.

4 When they are crunchy on the outside and tender inside, they are done. Mix mustard, chile, coriander, salt and onion salt. Sprinkle this over one batch of the chick-peas and toss lightly until the peas are thoroughly coated.

5 Mix the ginger, garlic salt and soy sauce and proceed in the same manner with the chick-peas in the other skillet. Serve hot in separate bowls.

Variation: *Try them as a garnish for soups or salads. Always serve them hot, by heating in a 250°F. oven for about 10 minutes.*

Maximum Recommended Freezer Storage: *6 months*

NACHOS
Cheese-Topped Corn Chips
24 chips

These tidbits are very popular in the Southwest as a snack or with Margaritas, frozen daiquiris or Mexican beer.

> 24 freshly fried Tostados (p. 32)
> salt
> 1 garlic clove, crushed
> 24 small squares of Monterey Jack, sharp Cheddar or jalapeño cheese
> 2 to 4 jalapeño chiles, finely chopped or thinly sliced into rings
> 4 scallions, tops included, finely chopped (optional)

1 Fry tostados, then shake in brown bag to which salt and garlic have been added.

2 Place tostados on a cookie sheet.

3 Top each one with a square of cheese, some chopped or sliced chile and some chopped scallion. Broil for 6 minutes, or until the cheese becomes bubbly. Serve hot.

Variations: *Top each piece of cheese with a spoon of sour cream or yogurt before adding chile. Or place a spoon of refritos or bean dip under the cheese.*

Not Recommended for Freezing

TASTY TORTILLAS
Cheese-Topped Corn Tortillas

6 tortillas

Tasty as a snack or as an accompaniment to soups or salads.

2 tablespoons butter
⅛ teaspoon salt
6 Corn Tortillas (p. 51)
6 slices of Cheddar cheese
2 tablespoons grated onion

1 Combine butter and salt. Spread on both sides of tortillas.

2 Place tortillas on a broiler rack and broil 5 inches from source of heat for about 4 minutes, or until crisp and brown. Turn.

3 Place 1 cheese slice on each tortilla, then sprinkle each with 1 teaspoon grated onion.

4 Broil until cheese bubbles, 3 to 5 minutes, or in microwave for about 1 minute. Serve warm.

Variations: *Use any sort of cheese; add chopped green chile, chile powder, refried beans, chorizo or any chile meat filling.*

Maximum Recommended Freezer Storage: *3 months in rigid cartons to prevent breaking*

EMPANADITAS
Baked Filled Pastries

about 24

Prepare snack empanaditas from any favorite, spicy filling. You will be amazed how well leftover bits of chile, beef or cheese can be transformed into delicious fillings for empanaditas. For conservation and convenience, freeze leftover fillings for "empanaditas-making day."

½ pound chorizo
2 to 4 tablespoons chopped green chile
¼ cup sour cream, or more
pastry for a 2-crust 9-inch pie

1 Fry the sausage and drain well. Combine with green chile to taste. Add sour cream to form a thick filling that will hold together.

2 Preheat oven to 400°F. Roll out the pastry as for pie. Using a round cutter, cut the pastry into rounds.

3 Place a spoonful of filling in the center of each pastry round, fold over, and seal with a forked or fluted edging.

4 Place turnovers on cookie sheets and bake until golden, about 15 minutes. Best served warm.

Note: *These can be frozen before or after baking. Frozen baked ones heat best in a foil-covered pan in a 400°F. oven. Heat for about 15 minutes.*
Maximum Recommended Freezer Storage: *1 month*

CHILE NUTS

These spicy nuts make a zesty addition to snack assortments, and are great served with icy cold beer or Margaritas. In the Southwest, you can purchase these already prepared; however, those you make are almost always the best. Even commercial chile nuts are improved by heating just before serving.

2 cups salted, skinless peanuts
2 tablespoons ground red chile (mild or hot, depending on your preference)
1 teaspoon onion powder
½ teaspoon garlic powder
few drops of vegetable oil (optional)

1 Preheat oven to 250°F. Place nuts in a large baking pan with sides. Sprinkle peanuts generously with all 3 spices. If seasonings will not stick, drizzle peanuts with a few drops of oil.

2 Heat in the oven for 15 minutes. Using a spatula, turn the peanuts over and bake for another 5 minutes. If "toastier" peanuts are desired, bake for a few minutes longer, watching carefully so as not to overroast. Serve warm by reheating briefly in a 250°F. oven for about 10 minutes.

Maximum Recommended Freezer Storage: *6 months*

TOSTADOS
Crisp-Fried Tortilla Quarters

48 tostados

These are good with most any kind of dip but indispensable with chile con queso and guacamole. Store any extras in the freezer.

1 quart lard or cooking oil, approximately
12 yellow, white or blue Corn Tortillas (p. 51)
1 garlic clove, crushed (optional)
salt
ground pure red chile (optional)

1 Heat lard or oil, 2 inches deep, in an electric deep-fryer, skillet or other heavy large pan. Using kitchen shears, cut the tortillas almost into quarters, leaving the center portion intact, pinwheel fashion (for ease in turning).

2 Fry the tortillas in deep fat until crisp, frying only one or two at a time.

3 Drain on absorbent paper toweling. Break into quarters. Combine garlic with salt in a brown bag and shake tostados to coat. Add chile if desired. Serve warm or at room temperature.

Maximum Recommended Freezer Storage: *6 months*

BEVERAGES

Along with the often spicy foods, gallons of beer, tequila, rum mixtures, California and Baja wines are traditionally imbibed.

Usually, a tequila drink is served before meals. Tequila is undoubtedly Mexico's most popular drink and has been widely adopted by Southwesterners. In addition to tequila in mixed drinks, true veterans enjoy it served simply by the shot with a half of lime and a saucer of coarse salt. To indulge, the lime is placed between the thumb and forefinger and a pinch of salt is placed on the thumb knuckle. Before each sip, a lick of salt is taken, then a suck of lime.

The favorite tequila drink is the Margarita, a lime-based drink, served in frosty, salt-rimmed glasses, with a touch of froth on top.

Daiquiris are a favorite alternative to Margaritas and are served slushy, almost frozen. Fruits such as peaches, bananas or strawberries are often added to make a delicious variation.

Native beer is generally drunk icy cold. For a switch, try a technique from Guadalajara as served in Mariachi Square. There, icy cold cans of beer (cerveza fria) are popularly garnished with a half of lime and coarse salt. Generally the lime has been squeezed around the rim of the can and the salt dusted on top. The flavor combination is somewhat similar to a Margarita. In fact, I've often called them a "poor man's Margarita."

Dry wines are good alongside a meal, as is Sangria. Both the traditional red or the newer white-wine version are served.

Kahlúa, a coffee-flavored liqueur, is native to Mexico and quite popular in drinks as well as a dessert ingredient.

MARGARITA

1 drink

These are the most traditional Mexican cocktails. The touch of froth added by the egg white is a recent twist.

> ½ ounce lime juice (juice of about 1 lime)
> salt
> ½ ounce Triple Sec
> 1½ ounces tequila
> ice

1 After lime juice is extracted, rub the lime rind around the edge of a chilled goblet or wineglass. Invert rim of glass onto a generously salted surface and rub the edge of the glass into salt so as to form a salty crust on the rim. If time permits, freeze the glasses to gain a frosty appearance.

2 Shake all ingredients together with ice or blend together in a blender.

3 Taste and add more lime or Triple Sec if desired.

4 Pour into the salt-rimmed glass.

Variation: *For an extra frothy Margarita, add about one-quarter of an egg white to the mixture before blending, and whip until frothy.*

Maximum Recommended Freezer Storage: *1 week*

TEQUILA SUNRISE

1 drink

A well-known, slightly sweeter tequila drink.

> juice and rind of ½ lime
> 2 ounces tequila
> 3 dashes of grenadine
> ½ teaspoon crème de cassis
> ice
> water

1 In a tall glass, place the lime juice and rind.

2 Add tequila, grenadine, crème de cassis and several ice cubes.

3 Fill the rest of the glass with water and stir thoroughly.

Variation: *Try sparkling water for a different taste. For a sweeter sunrise, add more grenadine.*

TEQUILA SOUR

1 drink

A tequila variation of the whiskey sour.

juice of ½ lemon
3 ounces tequila
1 ounce sugar syrup*
ice

1 Squeeze the lemon half into a pitcher or blender.
2 Add tequila, sugar syrup and 3 ice cubes.
3 Mix thoroughly.
4 Strain mixture into a sour glass.

*Make syrup by heating together 1 part sugar and 2 parts water; chill before using.

TEQUILA DAISY

1 drink

A sweeter version of the tequila sour.

2 ounces tequila
½ ounce fresh lemon juice (juice of about ½ lemon)
½ ounce grenadine syrup
ice

1 Combine tequila, lemon juice and grenadine in a blender or pitcher.
2 Add crushed ice and mix thoroughly.
3 Strain into a sour or cocktail glass.

TUCSON COCKTAIL

1 drink

2 ounces tequila
1 tablespoon honey
juice of ½ lime or lemon
ice

1 Combine tequila, honey and juice in a blender or shaker and mix well.
2 Pour into a cocktail glass with ice.

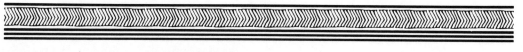

BLOODY MARIA

1 drink

This Southwestern version of a Bloody Mary is often served with brunch.

2 ounces tequila
6 ounces tomato juice
generous dash Worcestershire sauce
few drops hot pepper sauce
sprinkle of celery salt (optional)
ice cubes
1 long celery rib or strip of cucumber
1 lime slice

1 Follow the procedure in the Margarita recipe (p. 34) for salting the rims of glasses. Use large Mexican-type tumblers or stemmed glasses.
2 Mix tequila and Bloody Mary mix together in a salt-rimmed glass; add ice cubes.
3 Garnish with celery or cucumber and lime slice.

NEW MEXICAN FROZEN DAIQUIRIS

4 drinks

My favorite way to make super daiquiris.

⅔ cup light rum
3 ounces frozen limeade concentrate
6 ice cubes, or more

1 Place ingredients in the order listed in a blender.
2 Blend at high speed until you have a smooth mushy consistency.
3 Add more ice if you like a thicker drink.
4 Serve immediately.

Variation: *If a blender is not available, crush the ice very fine, and shake all ingredients vigorously in a shaker or jar.*
Maximum Recommended Freezer Storage: *1 week*

FROZEN PEACHY DAIQUIRIS 4 drinks

When making these, be prepared to make many. Most everyone seems to like the luscious fruity flavor.

⅔ cup light rum
3 tablespoons frozen limeade concentrate
1 fresh peach, or 3 tablespoons frozen sweetened peaches
6 ice cubes, or more

1 Place all ingredients in the order listed in a blender.
2 Blend at high speed until you have a smooth mushy consistency.
3 Serve immediately in old-fashioned glasses or long-stemmed goblets.

Variations: *Substitute frozen apricots, strawberries or fresh pineapple or fresh bananas.*
Maximum Recommended Freezer Storage: *1 week*

BLACK RUSSIAN 1 drink

1½ ounces Kahlúa
3 ounces vodka

1 Pour Kahlúa, then the vodka, into an old-fashioned glass with ice.
2 Stir gently.

MEXICAN GRASSHOPPER 1 drink

A slight twist to the traditional.

1 ounce Kahlúa
1 ounce green crème de menthe
1 ounce heavy cream
crushed ice

1 Pour the ingredients into a blender, then add crushed ice and blend thoroughly until frothy.
2 Serve in a chilled glass.

ANGEL'S KISS

1 drink

1 Fill any size liqueur glass about two-thirds full of Kahlúa.

2 Slowly pour heavy cream over the Kahlúa to make a thin layer of cream.

Variations: *Add ice and stir mixture together; or substitute milk for the cream before stirring. Blend the Kahlúa and cream together with ice in a blender for a frothy drink.*

SANGRÍA

6 drinks

Sangría has crossed all boundaries. Though it is great with Tex-Mex food, recently it seems to be accompanying almost any kind of cooking or party.

½ cup water
1 cup sugar
1 cinnamon stick
1 lemon, unpeeled
2 bananas, peeled
1 orange, peeled
ice
1 quart red wine

1 Boil water, sugar and cinnamon stick over medium-high heat for 5 minutes. Let the syrup cool and remove cinnamon stick.

2 Cut lemon, bananas and orange into thick slices and cover with the cooled syrup.

3 Chill for several hours.

4 Put ice in a glass pitcher and add the sliced fruit, half of the cinnamon syrup and the wine. Stir the mixture thoroughly, mashing the fruit slightly.

5 Serve the Sangría in well-chilled tumblers, garnishing each glass with some of the sliced fruit.

Note: *The remaining syrup can either be added to the pitcher to make a second quantity or reserved for adding fruit for later serving. Syrup will keep in the refrigerator for at least 1 month.*

Variations: *For Blond Sangría, substitute California Chablis or Spanish Rioja for the red wine.*

SQUEEZINS

1½ gallons

A great party punch for hot summer days, on the patio, at the beach or anywhere outdoors. You can vary the ingredients to suit your own taste and liquor supply.

2 quarts lemon-lime carbonated beverage
12 ounces frozen lemonade concentrate
6 ounces frozen limeade concentrate
1 quart club soda
1 quart light rum
1 pint dark rum or brandy
2 trays of ice

1 Combine all the ingredients in a large, deep punch bowl.
2 Stir until blended; chill.

Variations: *Pineapple or orange juice may be substituted for the lemonade and limeade. Vodka or gin may be substituted for the rums.*
Maximum Recommended Freezer Storage: *1 week*

SUNNY COOLER

1 drink

A spiked fruit drink.

ice cubes
2 ounces rum
juice of ½ lime
pineapple juice
1 lime slice

1 Fill a chilled tall glass with ice cubes.
2 Pour in the rum and lime juice, then add pineapple juice to fill glass; stir.
3 Garnish with a slice of lime.

MEXICAN COFFEE

Southwesterners have a great way with coffee; they spice a strong after-dinner brew with a hint of cinnamon.

> water
> dark roast coffee
> 1 teaspoon ground cinnamon for each 8 cups

1 Add cinnamon to the top of the coffee grounds, then brew coffee as usual.
2 Serve in earthenware or pottery mugs.

Variation: *Many like to serve dark brown sugar or piloncillo with the coffee, or to add about ½ cup to the pot before serving. Piloncillo is unrefined sugar, golden in color and with a more caramel flavor than granulated white sugar.*

NEW MEXICAN CHOCOLATE   12 drinks

A spicy version of traditional hot chocolate, which closely approximates the chocolate made from Mexican bar chocolate, presweetened and spiced.

> ½ cup sugar
> 2 tablespoons flour
> ¼ cup cocoa powder
> 1½ cups cold water
> ¼ teasoon salt
> 1 teaspoon ground cinnamon
> ¾ teaspoon ground cloves
> 6 cups milk
> 1 tablespoon vanilla extract

1 Combine sugar, flour, cocoa powder, water, salt and spices in a saucepan.
2 Cook over low heat until the ingredients combine in a smooth mixture. Over medium-high heat, simmer for about 4 minutes.
3 Slowly stir in the milk and heat until scalded, but do not boil.
4 Stir mixture until smooth. Add vanilla. If you are lucky enough to have a molinillo, Mexican chocolate stirrer, use it to whip the chocolate, otherwise beat with a fork.
5 Serve immediately in stemmed glasses or mugs.

Variation: *For fancy servings, decorate each mug with a cinnamon stick stirrer and a dollop of whipped cream dashed with nutmeg.*

SAUCES, PRESERVES & RELISHES

Sauces are the basis of this cuisine, creating the substance that both flavors and fills or binds the dishes together. Good examples are enchiladas where the sauce is the essence, as well as tamales, tacos and other less well known specialties.

Tex-Mex sauces are quite different from French or other European varieties in that the flavors are much more robust and can more easily be adjusted to suit your own palate. For example, if you prefer very mild red chile sauce, flavored with just a hint of pure Mexican orégano—fine! You will not be violating any basic rule of the cuisine if you make yours that way. Relishes and preserves, particularly the increasingly popular jalapeño jelly, are great treats for adding variation to Tex-Mex meals.

SALSA
Fresh Chile Sauce

about 2 cups

1 large fresh tomato, peeled
1 medium-size Bermuda onion or sweet purple Spanish onion, or 2 scallions, tops included
4 green chiles, parched (p. 21), or 4 ounces canned chopped green chiles
1 large or 2 small garlic cloves, minced
½ teaspoon salt

1 Chop the vegetables very fine.
2 Stir in the salt and allow to marinate for at least 15 minutes.

Note: *Salsa keeps for up to 1 week when refrigerated in a tightly closed container; or it can be frozen for later use in cooked sauces.*

Maximum Recommended Freezer Storage: *4 months*

SALSA VERDE
Green Chile Sauce

2 cups

This popular sauce can be varied in many ways.

1 tablespoon lard, butter or bacon drippings
½ cup chopped onion
2 tablespoons flour
2 cups canned stewed tomatoes, or 1½ cups chicken broth
1 cup chopped green chiles, or more
1 garlic clove, crushed
¾ teaspoon salt
dash of ground comino (optional)

1 Melt the lard in a saucepan over medium heat.
2 Sauté the chopped onion in the lard. Add the flour and mix well.
3 Add the stewed tomatoes or chicken broth, chopped chiles, garlic and seasonings. Simmer for 20 minutes. Serve as desired. To use in enchiladas, see Green Chile Enchiladas (p. 88).

Maximum Recommended Freezer Storage: *8 months*

SALSA VERDE, MEXICAN STYLE
Mexican Green Sauce   about 2 cups

Salsa verde is a traditional Mexican sauce used more frequently in California than in other border states. It is good over meats and as a sauce in tortilla concoctions such as tacos, burritos and the like. Tomatillos are generally available in Mexican specialty stores and should always be used; green tomatoes cannot be substituted, for they lack the sweet mild flavor.

½ medium onion, finely minced
1 tablespoon minced fresh cilantro
1 serrano or jalapeño chile, finely minced
½ teaspoon salt, or more
10 ounces canned tomatillos, well drained

1 If possible, use an electric blender or food processor to blend all the ingredients together. (Without machines, use a fork or mortar and pestle to mash the ingredients.)

2 Taste and adjust seasonings.

SALSA COLORADO
Very Hot Red Sauce   ½ cup

½ cup whole tomato sauce
1 teaspoon chile pequín, finely crushed, or more
1 teaspoon freshly squeezed lime juice
1 teaspoon cider vinegar
dash of ground Mexican orégano
1 garlic clove, freshly pressed
½ teaspoon ground comino

1 Place the tomato sauce in a small bowl, add remaining ingredients and stir.

2 Taste and adjust seasonings.

RED CHILE SAUCE

about 3 cups

The standby for many Southwestern menus; variations in seasonings can alter the sauce to suit your taste or the food you are enhancing. Serve over any main dish such as enchiladas, rellenos, burritos.

2 tablespoons lard or bacon drippings
2 tablespoons flour
¼ to ¾ cup ground red chile
2 cups cooled beef bouillon or water
up to 4 ounces tomato sauce (optional)
¾ teaspoon salt
1 garlic clove, crushed
pinch of ground Mexican orégano (optional)
dash of ground comino (optional)

1 Melt lard in a saucepan over low heat. Add the flour and stir until well mixed and slightly browned.

2 Add the smaller amount of chile to the bouillon or water, either when trying a new batch of chile or when preparing this recipe for the first time. Taste, then add more chile after the water is well mixed into the *roux*. Stir constantly when adding the water and continue to stir until a smooth sauce is obtained. Add tomato sauce, if desired (Tex-Mex cooks omit this). Slowly add it to the flour mixture, stirring constantly.

3 Season; taste and adjust the seasonings.

4 Simmer for at least 10 minutes, or longer, to develop the flavor.

Variations: *For enchiladas, 1 pound of ground beef can be browned and a chopped onion added when the beef is about half browned. Drain the excess fat and mix in the flour, omitting the shortening from the sauce recipe. Continue as above. When preparing the enchiladas, omit the raw onion if cooked onion has already been used. Cubed pork, chicken or other meat, fresh or leftover cooked, may be substituted for the beef.*

To substitute more the subtly flavored chile caribe, place the red chile in a thin layer in a shallow pan and roast in a 300°F. oven for 15 minutes, or until the color darkens. Then simmer 6 tablespoons of this roasted caribe in 1½ cups water for 30 minutes. Strain through a fine sieve. Use for chile-flavored liquid in the basic recipe, and reduce the bouillon by 1 cup.

Maximum Recommended Freezer Storage: *8 months*

GREEN CHILE RELISH

Green chiles, which have been parched and peeled (p. 21), may be made into a relish very easily.

1 Chop the chiles or work them with your hands to break the chiles into pieces. Be prepared for quite a burning sensation if you use your bare hands.

2 Season to taste with freshly minced garlic and salt for a delicious, zippy relish. This goes well with most any meat, cheese, egg or vegetable dish.

Maximum Recommended Freezer Storage: *8 months*

JALAPEÑO JELLY   5 jars, 1 cup each

At least three groups of women entrepreneurs recently developed successful businesses selling this jelly to specialty food markets. You can capture this same terrific flavor yourself. I always recommend making two recipes, one right after the other, preparing one mild and the other hot. Serve over a brick of cream cheese and spread on crackers. Also great served with any simply prepared meat dish such as roast leg of lamb, beef, pork or chicken.

3 large bell peppers, cored, seeded and finely chopped
3 medium-size jalapeño chiles for mild jelly, cored, seeded and finely chopped;
6 chiles for hot jelly
1½ cups cider vinegar
6½ cups sugar
6 ounces bottled liquid pectin

1 Scrub out five 1-cup jelly jars with resealable lids. Boil jars in water while preparing jelly.

2 Chop, blend or process the peppers and chiles. Combine with the vinegar and sugar in a large, heavy saucepan.

3 Bring to a boil and boil, stirring frequently, until the mixture becomes transparent, about 30 minutes.

4 Remove from heat and cool for about 10 minutes, then stir in the pectin.

5 Return to the heat and boil, stirring constantly, for 2 more minutes.

6 Remove from heat, skim, and ladle into the hot sterilized jars; seal at once.

7 In a large pan that will hold all the jars with space for water to circulate, place jars on a trivet. Add water to reach 1 inch over the tops of the lids. Boil for 15 minutes. Remove and cool.

Variation: *For a Christmas look that is great for gifts, prepare some recipes with red bell and chile peppers, and some with green bell peppers and chiles.*

RED CHILE JAM

3 jars, 1 cup each

A first cousin to jalapeño jelly, this jam is very good served with meats.

12 large fresh red chiles, New Mexico or California types
2 small lemons, quartered
½ cup apple cider vinegar
3 cups sugar

1 Remove seeds from chiles and chop finely, or process in a blender or food processor. Scrub out jars and boil.

2 Add lemons and vinegar to chiles and cook for about 30 minutes, or until chiles are well cooked. Remove lemon quarters and add sugar.

3 Boil for 10 minutes, or until jam reaches 9°F. above boiling or passes the sheet test. Spoon into sterilized jars and seal with paraffin.

PRICKLY PEAR JELLY

This jelly is a popular tourist item in the Southwest and is an unusual treat on tortillas or sopaipillas. Prickly pears are the rosy red fruits that develop on an Opuntia cactus.

prickly pear cactus fruits
water
¾ cup sugar per cup of juice
1 tablespoon lemon or orange juice per cup of juice

1 Carefully remove spines from prickly pear fruits. Wash them, cut into quarters and place in a kettle. Add enough water almost to cover.

2 Cook slowly until fruit is soft and reduced almost to a pulp. Pour into a jelly bag that has been moistened in hot water. Hang the bag over a large pot or bowl. Let drain overnight.

3 Heat juice to the boiling point and boil for 5 minutes. Remove scum. Measure the juice. Add ¾ cup sugar and 1 tablespoon lemon or orange juice for each cup of juice. Meanwhile scrub and sterilize 2 jelly jars for each cup of juice.

4 Cook mixture until syrup drops in sheets from a metal spoon, or until it reaches 9°F. above boiling. Pour into hot sterilized jars, cool, and cover with melted paraffin.

CHILES EN ESCABECHE
Pickled Chiles in Oil with Seasonings

10 pints

Either jalapeños or any type of green chiles can be used. These pickles are excellent for flavoring dishes such as guacamole or chile con queso. To use in these recipes, substitute the pickled chile (to taste) for the chile called for in the ingredients list.

30 pounds fresh green chiles, parched and peeled (p. 21) or unpeeled, scrubbed jalapeños
5 small white onions, sliced into ¼-inch rings
7 garlic cloves, minced
1 teaspoon ground Mexican orégano
4 small bay leaves
4 tablespoons salt
6 cups cider vinegar
5 cups distilled water
4 cups olive oil

1 Prepare chiles, leaving whole, but removing stems. Using a large heavy kettle, such as a 5-quart Dutch oven, place a small portion of the oil in the pan and heat until almost smoking. Then add the onions and garlic and cook until clear but not browned.

2 Meanwhile sterilize 10 pint-size canning jars in boiling water.

3 Add the orégano, bay leaves and salt and stir well to mix. Then add the vinegar and water and bring to a boil, stirring constantly.

4 When the salt has dissolved and the mixture is boiling, add the oil and bring to a boil again. Add the chiles and remove from heat. Fill the jars and seal, using canning lids, following conventional canning procedures.

SPANISH GREEN TOMATO PICKLES

2 quarts

1 peck or 2 gallons tomatoes
12 medium-size white onions, sliced
1 cup pickling or kosher salt
6 green peppers, cut into squares
2 tablespoons whole cloves
2 tablespoons whole allspice berries
1 tablespoon whole peppercorns
½ cup mustard seeds
2½ cups brown sugar
cider vinegar, 4% to 6% acidity

1 Use pear-shaped or round tomatoes. Wash, remove stem ends and blossom scars, and slice. Pack tomatoes and onions in alternate layers with salt sprinkled between layers. Let stand overnight. Drain.

2 Add green peppers, spices and sugar. Add vinegar almost to cover.

3 Heat gradually to boiling. Boil slowly for 30 minutes. Pour into sterilized jars and seal, following conventional canning procedures.

BREADS

Tortillas and sopaipillas are the "staffs of life" most frequently accompanying Tex-Mex meals. Tortillas are the best-known bread. Wheat-flour tortillas are generally served as a bread more often than the corn varieties.

Corn tortillas are the basis for many main dishes such as enchiladas, tacos and flautas. Serve them piping hot with generous quantities of butter for slathering on before folding them and sopping up extra sauce.

The secrets of sopaipillas recently began spreading like a prairie fire through the border states. Until recently they were known only in and around Albuquerque where they originated. The hollow inside, surrounded by a thin layer of golden crispy deep-fried bread, makes them a perfect recipient for generous quantities of honey. The combination of fried bread with sweet honey is a perfect counterpoint for calming down parched palates, seared by hot chiles. Even if the chile is not hot, the flavors are very complementary. The two foods that help most to calm down fiery dishes are fats and sugars. Fried foods, butter, milk, honey and jams are therefore some of the best accompaniments to spicy entrées.

Other more unusual but great-tasting breads are the Navajo fry bread and Indian bear claw bread. Fry bread is similar to sopaipillas, only it is not hollow. It is made in large rounds, perfect for serving as a bread or as a holder for fillings such as taco preparations. Bear claw bread is a crusty bread; if bought in the pueblos dotting the Rio Grande, it has a pungent piñon aroma coming from its being baked in *hornos*, the beehive-shaped outdoor ovens to be found in every New Mexico native's backyard.

TORTILLA TIPS

Corn tortillas are the basis of many Tex-Mex dishes and are often served as a bread accompaniment to meals. Homemade tortillas are superior to the commercially prepared ones. Wheat-flour tortillas are rolled and baked similarly but have an entirely different flavor. They are more of a specialty, usually used for burritos, soft tacos and huevos rancheros. They are great for sopping up.

The major ingredient of corn tortillas is masa, a soft flour made from cornmeal treated with limewater. My favorite is blue cornmeal, the Northern Rio Grande specialty of the Pueblo Indians, but it is difficult to obtain.

You can buy either dry or prepared (already moistened) masa. Mexican food stores, tortilla or tamale factories sell the prepared masa. Only freshly prepared masa works for tortillas. If you want to buy in quantity, masa can be frozen to make tamales, but not tortillas. In the refrigerator masa will keep fresh for only 2 to 3 days. Most masa is made from white corn; however, if you are lucky enough to shop in New Mexico, perhaps you can savor blue cornmeal.

Dry masa is most used. It requires only moistening, as described in the following recipe. The most broadly distributed brand is prepared by Quaker Oats and is sold under the name of "Masa Harina."

Tortilla techniques take a while to master. Tips for good results are to use very warm water, mix the dough well, then let it rest for 20 to 60 minutes. Roll out the dough on a water-sprinkled surface between sheets of wax paper or moist cloths, whichever is best for you. A tortilla press is much easier to use. Always fry on a medium-hot surface which has been well rubbed with lard and wiped dry to prevent sticking. When learning to make tortillas, for easier handling and a slightly different flavor, you may wish to substitute flour for one third of the masa when making the dough.

At 0°F. frozen tortillas will keep for several months with little or no loss of flavor. To use, simply separate the number you wish to use and place them on the counter for a few minutes. Then use as desired. Be sure to remove any ice crystals and to blot any moisture before frying or heating them to prevent spattering and soggy spots.

To serve, heat foil-wrapped tortillas in a moderate oven, or fry in medium-hot fat and drain.

CORN TORTILLAS

about 12 tortillas

2 cups masa harina (white, yellow or blue)
1 teaspoon salt
boiling water

1 Mix the salt into the masa and make a well in the center. Pour about ½ cup water into the well. Mix, then continue adding water, a little at a time, until a very firm dough is formed. (I find mixing the dough at first with a spoon and finishing with my hands yields the best dough.) The dough should be very firm and springy when touched, not dry and crumbly nor sticky.

2 Let dough set, covered, for about 1 hour.

3 Preheat a griddle or other flat surface that is well seasoned. Do not add any shortening. Divide the dough into balls, each about 2 inches in diameter.

4 To form tortillas, Mexicans use their moistened palms; however, most of the rest of us find a rolling pin, a bollito or a tortilla press easier. Roll the dough between 2 moistened pieces of wax paper or soft cloths. Be especially careful when moistening the wax paper to sprinkle only a few drops of water on each piece. If you have trouble making round tortillas, trim the edges.

5 Peel off 1 piece of the wax paper. Then place the tortilla on the hot surface and peel the wax paper off the second as the tortilla begins to heat. When the tortilla is hot on the top, turn on the second side for a few seconds. Stack in a warm cloth.

6 As a bread, serve warm, flat, folded in quarters, or rolled. Or fry for enchiladas or other uses.

Freezing Hints: *Leftovers can be packaged in freezer-weight plastic bags or other freezer packaging material.*

Maximum Recommended Freezer Storage: *3 months*

TORTILLAS DE HARINA
Wheat-Flour Tortillas
8 to 12 tortillas

Wheat-flour tortillas are the daily bread in the border states. They are a great accompaniment to almost any dish containing chile and are the basis for burritos.

4 cups all-purpose flour
2 teaspoons salt
2 teaspoons baking powder
½ teaspoon sugar (creates a browner bubbled surface)
4 tablespoons lard or butter
1½ cups warm water

1 Combine dry ingredients, then cut in the lard (butter will not yield as tender tortillas nor as traditional a flavor) with a pastry blender or your fingers.

2 Add the warm water, a few drops at a time, and work dough with your hands until manageable.

3 Knead the dough 15 to 20 times, then allow it to stand for 10 minutes.

4 Form the dough into balls the size of an egg, then roll them with a bollito or small rolling pin until they are about 6 inches in diameter and about ⅛ inch thick.

5 If possible, use a hot cast-iron griddle or stove lid. A regular griddle or frypan can be used, but the tortillas will not brown as well. Cook each tortilla until it has light brown flecks on each side.

Note: *Use lard or butter only; vegetable shortening makes them tough.*

Maximum Recommended Freezer Storage: *3 months*

SOPAIPILLAS
Deep-Fried Bread

4 dozen

These hollow "sofa pillows" of bread are immediate favorites of all those who try them. They are easy to make if the fat is very hot and only a few are fried at a time. History reveals they originated in Old Town, Albuquerque, about 300 years ago.

4 cups sifted all-purpose flour
1½ teaspoons salt
1 teaspoon baking powder
1 tablespoon lard or butter
1 package active dry yeast (optional)
¼ cup warm water (105° to 115°F.)
1¼ cups scalded milk, approximately
1 quart lard or cooking oil

1 Combine dry ingredients and cut in 1 tablespoon lard.

2 Dissolve yeast in the water. Add yeast to scalded milk, cooled to room temperature. If not using yeast, use 1½ cups milk; omit the ¼ cup warm water.

3 Make a well in the center of dry ingredients. Add about 1¼ cups liquid to dry ingredients and work into dough. Add more liquid until dough is firm and springy and holds its shape, similar to a yeast dough.

4 Knead dough 15 to 20 times, then invert the bowl over the dough and set aside for approximately 10 minutes. Heat 1 quart lard or oil to 420°F. in a deep-fryer.

5 Roll one fourth of the dough to ¼-inch thickness or slightly thinner, then cut into squares or triangles; do not reroll any of the dough. Cover the cut dough with a towel as you fry the sopaipillas, a few at a time, in the hot fat. They should puff up and become hollow very soon after being dropped into the fat. To assure puffing, slightly stretch each piece of dough before lowering it into the fat, then place the rolled or top side of dough into the fat first, so it will be the bottom side. Hold each piece of dough down in the fat until it puffs.

6 Drain sopaipillas on absorbent toweling. Serve as a bread with any Southwestern meal. They are specially good served with honey.

Variations: *Sopaipillas may be dusted with a sugar-cinnamon mixture to be served as a dessert with New Mexican Chocolate (p. 40).*
Stuff hot large sopaipillas with refried beans, chile con carne, chopped onion, grated cheese and lettuce or guacamole for a main dish at luncheon.

Freezing Hint: *Any remaining sopaipillas can be frozen. To serve, heat in a foil packet in a 350°F. oven for about 15 minutes. Just before serving, open the foil so that the sopaipillas will dry out on the outside.*

Maximum Recommended Freezer Storage: *3 months*

NAVAJO FRY BREAD

about 1 dozen pieces

This mainstay of the Navajo diet is a popular attraction at most fairs and outdoor summer shows in New Mexico. It is not unusual to see people lined up for almost a block to wait their turn to get some freshly made fry bread. This is the traditional recipe; however, the Indians make it in various ways, sometimes using all cornmeal instead of wheat flour and sometimes adding wild berries, seeds or nuts during the summer to add variety. The Navajo take this bread with them while out herding sheep and goats.

lard or oil
2 cups all-purpose flour, unsifted
4 teaspoons baking powder
1 teaspoon salt
⅔ cup warm water or more
cornmeal

1 Put enough melted lard or oil in a deep-fryer to reach a depth of 2 to 3 inches. Heat lard or oil (lard is traditional) to 400°F.

2 Combine flour, baking powder and salt. Add ½ cup warm water and continue adding water to reach the consistency of bread dough; more water may be needed.

3 Tear off balls of dough. Roll out balls on a board lightly dusted with cornmeal or flour until each is ¼ inch thick. Punch a hole in the center of each piece; the hole is a traditional mark of fry bread and comes from the Navajo custom of sticking a branch into the bread and lowering it into the hot oil.

4 Fry 1 bread at a time, turning each as soon as it becomes golden. Drain on absorbent paper and serve hot with honey or dusted with powdered sugar.

Variations: *Fry bread makes a delicious taco and is good as a bread with most chile dishes.*

Maximum Recommended Freezer Storage: *3 months*

ISLETA BREAD
Indian Yeast Bread
(sometimes called Bear Claw or Paw Bread)

2 loaves

The Indian women living in pueblos dotting the Rio Grande in New Mexico bake a marvelous bread that is crusty and reminiscent of good French bread. The traditional Indian way to make the bread is to start the afternoon before planning to bake. The yeast, water and flour are stirred together and allowed to ferment overnight. They use only ½ package of yeast to each 12½ pounds of flour. The next morning, the rest of the ingredients are added to the dough.

Mrs. Carolyn Olguin of Isleta kindly shared her recipe with me. This yields marvelous bread. I adapted the recipe so that it does not require a day and a half to prepare. (I must admit that when she gave me the recipe, it was a shock to learn that it started with a 50-pound bag of flour!) On baking day, shortly after kneading the bread, she goes outside to her horno (an adobe oven) and builds a large piñón wood fire. In the afternoon, when the bread is ready for baking, she scrapes the coals out of the oven. With a large paddle, she places the loaves in the oven to bake for about 1½ hours. And it is worth the trouble!

1 package active dry yeast
¼ cup warm water (105° to 115°F.)
½ teaspoon lard
¼ teaspoon honey
¼ teaspoon salt
1 cup hot water
5 cups all-purpose flour

1 Dissolve the yeast in the water; set aside. Measure the lard, honey and salt into a large mixing bowl. Add the hot water and stir to dissolve well.

2 When the lard mixture has cooled to room temperature, combine it with the yeast mixture. Add the flour, 1 cup at a time, beating well after each addition.

3 When 4 cups flour have been added to the dough, spread remaining 1 cup flour on a board or counter and on it knead the dough until smooth and elastic, about 15 minutes.

4 Let dough rise in a bowl in a warm place until doubled; be sure you have covered the dough with a sheet of wax paper and a towel. When dough is doubled, turn it out onto a lightly floured surface and knead again.

5 Divide dough into 2 equal parts and shape each into a flat circle about 8 inches in diameter. Fold each circle almost in half, allowing the bottom half to extend about 1 inch beyond the top.

6 Using a sharp knife, slash the dough twice, cutting through both parts of the dough, about halfway back to the fold. This will create 3 separated sections, or the bear's claw. Transfer the dough to a greased 9-inch pie plate, curving the folded portion to create a crescent effect. Separate the slashes, forming the claw or paw effect. Cover. Allow to double in a warm place.

7 Preheat oven to 350°F. and place a shallow pan of water on the bottom rack of the oven. Place the loaves in the oven so that neither is directly above the water. Bake for 1 hour, or until lightly browned. Serve hot or cold.

Note: *The shape described is called a "bear claw." Indian bread from the Pueblos always is made in this shape.*

Maximum Recommended Freezer Storage: *3 months*

MOYETTES
Cinnamon-Sugar Crusted Sweet Bread   8 to 10 small loaves

Once when I was responsible for the refreshments for an elegant merienda (afternoon tea), sponsored by the Women's Committee of the Greater Albuquerque Chamber of Commerce, I asked my Kitchen Attendant from Public Service Company of New Mexico to bake some of her delicious Bizcochitos (p.164) and some Buñuelos (p. 164). She said she felt buñuelos were too sweet and gooey to serve at a fine tea such as I was planning, but the other ladies on my committee insisted on them. So she made both.

On the day of the merienda I noticed many small loaves of breadlike rolls individually wrapped in wax paper. Before taking them to the merienda, I asked her what they were. She replied that she thought the ladies might like to try some moyettes, her favorite accompaniment to coffee, tea or New Mexican Chocolate (p. 40).

This is the recipe she used and they turned out to be the favorite food at the merienda. My complete menu was bizcochitos, buñuelos, moyettes, assorted fresh fruit plates, piñon nuts, coffee and New Mexican chocolate. The guests were all newcomers to our city and were enthralled with the delightful goodies that they had neither seen nor heard of before. To complete the setting, we served the merienda in a large rambling adobe house and used serving dishes of New Mexican pottery.

5 cups sifted all-purpose flour
2 cups sugar
pinch of salt
3 tablespoons butter or oil
1 package active dry yeast (use 2 packages if time is short)
1 cup warm water (105° to 115°F.)
1 egg, slightly beaten
2 teaspoons anise extract or ¼ cup aniseeds
½ cup melted butter
2 teaspoons ground cinammon

1 Sift flour, 1 cup sugar and salt together. Cut in the butter until the mixture resembles coarse meal. If using oil, stir oil into liquid ingredients after adding the egg.

2 Dissolve yeast in warm water, stir vigorously, and allow to ferment for 5 to 10 minutes. Then add the egg and anise extract or aniseeds.

3 Add a small quantity of the flour mixture to the yeast and beat until thoroughly blended. Let stand for a few minutes, or until dough becomes light and airy.

4 Add the rest of the flour mixture, adding more flour if necessary to make a stiff dough. Knead on a lightly floured board until satiny.

5 Butter the top of the dough, cover with wax paper and let rise until doubled.

6 When the bread has risen, punch it down, and let it rise until doubled again.

7 Knead the dough slightly, then form into balls the size of an orange. With a rolling pin, flatten to ½ to ¾ inch thick.

8 Prepare a topping by mixing together the melted butter, remaining 1 cup sugar and the cinnamon. Spread topping on all sides of the rolls.

9 Let rolls rise until light and about doubled in size. When nearly doubled, preheat oven to 400°F.

10 Bake in the preheated oven for 20 to 25 minutes, or until golden. Slice thinly and butter generously with soft butter. Arrange slices on a platter as desired. They will keep for 2 to 3 days at room temperature when well wrapped.

Maximum Recommended Freeezer Storage: *3 months*

SOUTHWESTERN CORN BREAD

9 to 12 servings

This tasty corn bread is extra hearty; serve with a main-dish salad or stew for a delicious combination. The bread's moist quality makes it a favorite with campers and picnickers.

1 cup blue or yellow cornmeal
1 tablespoon baking powder
1½ teaspoons salt
2 eggs
⅔ cup melted butter or bacon drippings
1 cup sour cream
2 cups cooked corn kernels
¼ pound Monterey Jack or Cheddar cheese, grated
4 ounces canned chopped green chiles
½ cup bacon bits (optional)

1 Preheat oven to 375°F. Grease a 9-inch-square pan or large cast-iron skillet.

2 Mix dry ingredients together and make a well in the center. Add eggs, butter and sour cream and blend thoroughly. Fold in corn kernels.

3 Pour half of the batter into the prepared pan. Cover with grated cheese and chiles.

4 Pour remaining batter over top. Add bacon bits if desired. Bake in the preheated oven for 30 to 40 minutes.

Maximum Recommended Freezer Storage: *2 months*

BOLILLOS
Mexican Hard Rolls

3 dozen hard rolls

Once you make these easy-to-do rolls, you will find yourself baking them again and again.

1 package active dry yeast
2 teaspoons sugar
1¾ cups warm water (105° to 115°F.)
1 teaspoon salt
6 cups sifted all-purpose flour

1 Stir yeast and sugar together, then dissolve in warm water.

2 Add the salt, then the flour, 2 cups at a time, beating well after each addition. After adding the fifth cup of flour, add flour slowly until the dough becomes too stiff to handle.

3 Turn out onto a lightly floured board and knead until satiny. Place in a lightly greased bowl, being sure to grease the top of the bread, then cover with a sheet of wax paper and a towel.

4 Let rise in a warm place free of drafts until doubled in bulk. When dough is doubled, punch down and allow to double again.

5 Form into long slender rolls, twisting each end. Some like to roll the dough into very long ropes about 2 inches in diameter and snip off 3- to 4-inch pieces of dough, twisting each end. For authentic-looking rolls, they should be rather flat with twisted ends. Lay rolls about 2 inches apart on a lightly floured baking sheet.

6 After shaping the rolls, gash the tops with a sharp knife or scissors. Cover with a towel and again allow to double in bulk. When nearly doubled, preheat oven to 400°F. and lightly oil the tops of the rolls.

7 Bake for 30 to 40 minutes, until lightly browned. Serve piping hot with lots of butter.

Maximum Recommended Freezer Storage: *3 months*

SOUPS & STEWS

Soups are a predictable beginning to any meal, yet in Tex-Mex country they are relatively new and have only recently become popular. They have yet to become as traditional as in Mexico.

In Old Mexico, soup is served two ways—wet and dry. Wet soups are the same as our traditional soups. The dry variety, *sopa seca*, are basically rice, hominy or other heavy, starchy grain dishes which are served as a course after the wet soup. In simpler meals the dry soups are served as a side dish with meat, seafood or eggs. I have never been able to find out why they are called soups, for they cannot be considered such in accordance with other cuisines.

Chilaquiles comes the closest to being a *sopa seca*. The soups in this chapter other than the chilaquiles range from hearty such as the chile stew to light and soupy and are all "wet."

GAZPACHO I

8 servings

Gazpacho is one of the best ways to start or finish a Mexican meal. Smoothly textured, subtly flavored and icy cold, this favorite rates rave reviews as a starter to whet the appetite or as a cool-down after a spicy, main course.

1 cup tomato juice
1 tablespoon wine vinegar
3 tablespoons olive oil
1 garlic clove, crushed
¼ teaspoon salt, or more
1 medium-size Spanish onion, peeled and quartered
4 large very ripe tomatoes, peeled and chopped
1 large cucumber, peeled and chopped
1 green pepper (bell or chile, depending upon taste preference), seeded and quartered
1 teaspoon minced cilantro
freshly ground black pepper

1 Place tomato juice, wine vinegar, olive oil, garlic, salt and onion in a blender or food processor and mix for a few seconds.

2 Add remaining ingredients and blend until a smooth texture is obtained. You can also finely chop the remaining ingredients and stir together. Season with a few grinds of black pepper and more salt, if desired, and chill for at least 1 hour before serving.

3 Serve in small glasses, bowls or goblets lined with lettuce leaves.

Not Recommended for Freezing

GAZPACHO II

6 to 8 servings

In this variation each guest has the opportunity to custom tailor his seasonings, making this one particularly good for small luncheons or dinners.

5 red ripe tomatoes, quartered
1 sweet onion, quartered
1 garlic clove, crushed
1 cup beef stock, cooled
3 tablespoons olive oil
2 tablespoons vinegar
2 tablespoons minced fresh parsley (do not substitute dry; if fresh is unavailable, omit)

½ teaspoon ground mild red chile
salt
1 cucumber, peeled
1 bell pepper
4 scallions, tops included
4 thick slices of French bread, cut into cubes

1 In a blender or a food processor, place tomatoes, onion, garlic, stock, olive oil, vinegar and 1 tablespoon of the parsley.

2 Process until all ingredients are reduced to a lumpy purée. Add the red chile and salt to taste.

3 Chill for at least 2 hours before serving.

4 Meanwhile, chop the cucumber and bell pepper into fine cubes. Thinly slice the scallions. Place vegetables in similar pottery bowls.

5 Toast the bread cubes in a 300°F. oven for about 30 minutes, or until golden. Cool cubes and place in another pottery bowl.

6 To serve, place the gazpacho in pottery soup bowls or mugs. Top each serving with some of the reserved minced parsley. Invite guests to add the desired quantity of vegetables and croutons to their servings.

SOPA DE ELOTE
Corn Soup

6 servings

1 onion, finely chopped
2 tablespoons butter
2½ cups cooked corn kernels
5 cups chicken stock
1 large green pepper
salt
freshly ground pepper
1 cup heavy cream

1 Sauté the onion in the butter until onion's translucent.

2 Blend 2 cups of the corn, the onion and 1 cup of the stock in a blender or food processor until you have a smooth purée.

3 Combine remaining stock, green pepper and the purée in a saucepan. Season with salt and pepper to taste and cook over low heat for 10 minutes.

4 Whisk cream into soup, then bring soup to a boil.

5 Serve immediately, garnished with the reserved corn.

Variation: *Whip ½ cup heavy cream with ⅛ teaspoon salt until stiff. Place a dollop of cream on each bowl of soup and sprinkle with ground red chile.*

SOPA DE AGUACATE
Creamy Cold Avocado Soup

6 to 8 servings

3 large ripe avocados, cold from refrigerator
salt
freshly ground pepper
1 teaspoon ground mild red chile
¼ teaspoon freshly grated nutmeg
1 cup cold heavy cream
6 cups chicken stock
½ cup dry sherry

1 Peel and pit avocados. Place in a blender or food processor and purée, or mash with a fork until smooth. Season with salt and pepper to taste. Add chile and nutmeg.

2 Beat the cream into the avocado mixture.

3 Heat the chicken stock and sherry together over medium heat for 5 minutes. Set aside and allow to cool.

4 When stock is cool, pour over avocado mixture. Refrigerate for at least 4 hours to allow flavors to blend.

Variation: *To serve hot, start with room temperature avocados blended with cream and seasonings. Pour hot chicken stock and sherry over avocado mixture, blend well, and serve immediately.*

SOPA MEXICANA
Mexican Vegetable Soup

10 servings

1 stewing chicken, 3 pounds, cut up
5 cups water
1 medium-size onion, chopped
2 celery ribs, chopped
1 teaspoon salt
freshly ground pepper
6 large tomatoes, cut up
2 medium-size carrots, thinly sliced
1 medium-size purple Spanish onion, cut into ¼-inch-thick slices and separated into rings
3 large ears of corn, each cut into 3 pieces
1 small zucchini, thinly sliced
1 small avocado, peeled, pitted and cut into long pieces

1 Combine chicken, water, onion, celery, salt and pepper to taste in a large pot or Dutch oven. Bring to a boil, reduce heat and simmer covered for 2 hours, or till chicken is tender.

2 Remove chicken and skim fat off broth. Strain broth, discarding all vegetables. Return strained broth to the pot.

3 Add tomatoes, carrots and onion rings to broth. Cover and simmer for 30 minutes, or until carrots are tender.

4 Meanwhile, debone and skin chicken. Dice chicken and add to broth along with corn and zucchini. Cover and simmer for 10 to 15 minutes, or until vegetables are tender.

5 Serve with a garnish of avocado slices.

MEXICAN POTATO SOUP   6 servings

3 bacon strips, cut into small strips
3 large or medium-size potatoes, peeled and cubed
5 cups water or more
1 cup tomato sauce
¼ cup chopped onion
1½ teaspoons salt
10 ounces canned whole or chopped green chiles
½ pound sharp cheese, grated

1 Brown the bacon in a large kettle. Add the potato cubes and stir until they are coated with drippings.

2 Add the water, tomato sauce, onion and salt. Reduce heat to a simmer and cook for 1 hour.

3 Place the green chiles and grated cheese in 6 soup bowls. Spoon hot soup over them. Serve.

Variation: *Minced garlic can be added to taste.*

Not Recommended for Freezing

GREEN CHILE STEW

6 to 8 servings

Great served with wheat-flour tortillas.

24 fresh or canned green chiles
2 pounds roast pork (shoulder or butt), cubed
¼ cup flour
2 tablespoons bacon drippings
2 large onions, finely chopped
6 large tomatoes, peeled, seeded and chopped, or 3 cups stewed tomatoes
6 ounces canned tomato paste
2 cups water
2 garlic cloves, crushed
2 teaspoons salt

1 If chiles are fresh, parch and peel them (p. 21), removing the ribs, seeds and tops.

2 Flour the pork and brown it in the drippings in a skillet. Remove pork to a large stewing pot, 3- to 5-quart size. Add the onions to the fat remaining in the skillet and cook until onion is translucent.

3 Add onions to the pork. Cut the chiles into 1-inch slices; add to the meat and onions in the pot.

4 Add remaining ingredients and cook over medium heat for about 1 hour, until the stew is slightly thickened.

Maximum Recommended Freezer Storage: *3 months*

CHILAQUILES
Baked Tortillas in Tomato-Chile Sauce

4 to 5 servings

A popular breakfast or lunch dish that is great for using leftover tortillas. For breakfast, a poached egg nestled atop each serving is good. Garnish with shredded Monterey Jack cheese if desired.

10 Corn Tortillas (p. 51)
cooking oil
2 large or 4 medium tomatoes, cut into thin wedges
1 small onion, chopped
1 garlic clove, crushed
1 green chile, chopped, or more
dash of salt
pinch of ground comino

1 Cut the tortillas into 2-inch squares. Fry briefly in hot oil, being sure they do not become crisp. Drain well.

2 Combine all the ingredients with the tortilla pieces in a saucepan. Simmer for about 5 minutes. Serve immediately.

Not Recommended for Freezing

SOPA DE TORTILLAS
Tortilla Soup

4 to 8 servings

A hearty soup that can be a main dish for lunch or a starter preceding dinner.

1 tablespoon minced onion
1 garlic clove, crushed
2 tablespoons bacon drippings or lard
2 cups beef stock
3 whole dried Anaheim or other mild chiles, crushed (¼ cup crushed or caribe chile)
¼ teaspoon ground comino
¼ cup grated Monterey Jack cheese
4 cups crisp tostados

1 Sauté the onion and garlic in the bacon drippings or lard in a medium-size saucepan.

2 Add the stock, chiles and comino and simmer until the chiles are tender, about 30 minutes.

3 Ladle the soup into bowls or mugs and top each bowl with some of the grated cheese. Divide about half of the tostados evenly among the servings. Heat the bowls under the broiler for about 5 minutes to melt the cheese.

4 Sprinkle a few more tostados on each. Serve remaining tostados separately in a bowl.

SALADS

Salads are relatively recent additions to Tex-Mex meals and are largely credited to the creative touches supplied by contemporary cooks in the westernmost states, particularly California. There, avocados, lettuce, cheese, tomatoes, olives, various, meat-laden sauces and beans or other hearty vegetables have been combined with wild abandon, resulting in colorful main-dish salads. Other Tex-Mex salads are marinated or pickled vegetables or fruit salads.

Traditionally, generous garnishes of lettuce, tomatoes and other fresh vegetables or guacamole are all that is needed to accompany most Tex-Mex dishes.

TOSTADOS COMPUESTAS
Crisp-Fried Tortilla Topped with Salad

6 servings

This is the Southwest's version of a main-dish salad.

Meat Sauce (recipe follows)
2 cups Frijoles Refritos (p. 154)
several dashes of hot-pepper sauce
3 scallions, sliced
salt
6 corn tortillas, fried crisp and left flat
6 ounces Monterey Jack cheese, cut into strips
Salad Mixture (recipe follows)
1 medium-size avocado, sliced into thin strips
1 cup shredded sharp Cheddar cheese
Salsa Verde (p. 42)

1 Prepare meat sauce and keep warm. Combine the beans with hot-pepper sauce and the chopped scallions. Add salt to taste.

2 Place a crisp-fried tortilla on each of 6 pottery plates. Spread some bean mixture on each and top with strips of Jack cheese, evenly dividing each ingredient. Preheat oven to 350°F.

3 Top the bean mixture with the meat sauce and heat for 30 minutes.

4 To serve, arrange salad on each. Garnish with the avocado strips, shredded Cheddar and some salsa verde.

MEAT SAUCE

1 pound beef stewing meat, cut into tiny cubes
1 tablespoon fat
1 onion, finely chopped
2 garlic cloves, minced
1¼ cups Red Chile Sauce (p. 44)
½ teaspoon salt

1 Brown the beef in the fat over medium heat. As meat starts to brown, add onion and garlic. Cook until onion is translucent.

2 Add the red chile sauce and salt, and simmer until flavors blend, 1 to 2 hours. Serve hot over the bean mixture.

SALAD MIXTURE

3 scallions, sliced
12 pitted ripe olives, sliced
1 large tomato, cut into thin wedges
salt
2 cups finely shredded lettuce

1 Combine all ingredients just before serving. Season lightly with salt. Spoon on top of the meat sauce. Garnish and serve.

Variation: *Serve these buffet style, with the mixtures in bowls, and let guests prepare their own. Restaurants frequently serve these with the bottom tortilla formed into a cup. The ingredients are then added in the same order.*

Not Recommended for Freezing

PICKLED COLESLAW   about 2 quarts

Coleslaw, especially the pickled variety, is often served with Southwestern foods. This particular slaw is a wonderful "take-along" for campers and picnickers because it keeps very well without refrigeration. The story goes that it keeps for 9 days, but I've never had any last that long!

1 cup salad oil
1 cup white or cider vinegar
1¼ to 1½ cups sugar
2 tablespoons celery seeds
lettuce leaves (optional)
3 pounds cabbage, chopped
1 medium-size green pepper, finely chopped
2 medium-size white onions, finely chopped
1 tablespoon salt
½ teaspoon freshly ground black pepper

1 Heat the oil, vinegar, sugar and celery seeds until the mixture boils and the sugar dissolves. Simmer for a few minutes.

2 Combine the chopped vegetables in a large bowl. Season with the salt and pepper and mix well. Pour hot dressing over the vegetables and let stand for at least 2 hours before serving. Better yet, chill overnight for best flavor. Serve on top of lettuce leaves, if desired.

MARINATED VEGETABLE SALAD WITH BLUE-CHEESE DRESSING

4 servings

The sweet Spanish onions make the salad extra delightful, so be sure to try the salad when they are in season.

4 large tomatoes
2 cucumbers, scored with a fork
1 large sweet purple Spanish onion
Blue-Cheese Dressing (recipe follows)
4 large lettuce leaves

1 Cut the tomatoes into thin wedges. Slice cucumbers with skin on. Cut the onion crosswise into thin slices and separate slices into rings.

2 Pour on dressing 1 or more hours ahead of serving time, toss together and refrigerate. Do not discard excess dressing; save for use over a tossed salad.

3 Stir vegetables with dressing, then place on lettuce leaves. Serve.

BLUE-CHEESE DRESSING

1¼ cups dressing

¾ cup salad oil (use ¼ cup olive and ½ cup salad oil for best flavor)
¼ cup wine or tarragon vinegar
1 small garlic clove, crushed
1 teaspoon salt
generous grind of black pepper
3 tablespoons crumbled blue cheese, or more

1 Blend ingredients except cheese together, using an electric blender or a mixer. Add blue cheese to taste.

2 Pour over the vegetables or use over any salad.

MEXICALI SALAD

4 to 6 servings

This California-inspired salad is great for buffets. I like to serve it with Buffet Tamale Pie (p. 108) or Enchilada Casserole (p. 86). Also, it is a good way to use leftover guacamole.

2 cups vinegar and oil salad dressing (your favorite well-seasoned dressing, or the recipe that follows)
½ cup sliced hearts of palm
4½ ounces pitted ripe olives, halved crosswise
3 scallions, chopped
2 dozen cherry tomatoes, halved
1 large head of romaine lettuce
1 large avocado
2 garlic cloves, crushed
1 teaspoon lime juice
1 green chile, chopped
¼ teaspoon salt
½ cup sour cream
freshly ground black pepper
3 tablespoons toasted sesame seeds
1 cup tostados

1 The day before serving the salad, prepare the salad dressing and set aside.

2 Place the hearts of palm, two-thirds of the sliced olives, the chopped scallions and cherry tomatoes in a large jar or plastic container. Add enough salad dressing to cover, then shake ingredients together and refrigerate.

3 During the morning before planning to serve the salad, rinse the romaine and tear into medium-size pieces. Refrigerate until ready to use.

4 Prepare guacamole, using your favorite recipe or by combining the avocado, garlic, lime juice, green chile and salt. Thin with sour cream to the consistency of mayonnaise.

5 About 5 minutes before serving, sprinkle lettuce with freshly ground black pepper and toasted sesame seeds. Add the marinated vegetables and the marinade and toss together. Arrange salad in a large serving bowl.

6 Place the guacamole in the center of the salad. Encircle the guacamole with the rest of the black olives. Top the salad with the tostados and serve.

VINEGAR AND OIL SALAD DRESSING

2 cups

1½ cups olive or salad oil
½ cup red wine vinegar
1 teaspoon sugar
1 tablespoon tomato paste
½ teaspoon salt
¼ teaspoon ground Mexican orégano
freshly ground black pepper to taste

1 Place all ingredients in a small deep bowl and whisk together until foamy and well mixed. Taste and adjust seasonings.

SANTA FE SALAD

4 to 6 servings

1 pound ground beef, browned
1 small onion, chopped
2 cups cooked kidney beans, drained
½ cup Vinegar and Oil Salad Dressing (p. 71)
½ cup water
1 tablespoon ground red chile
2 garlic cloves, minced
salt
4 to 6 tortillas
fat or oil
1 quart coarsely chopped lettuce
2 cups coarsely chopped romaine or red-leaf lettuce or endive
½ cup coarsely shredded purple cabbage
½ cup sliced scallions
1 cup cherry tomatoes, halved
2 cups grated Cheddar or Monterey Jack cheese
1 avocado, cut into long, thin slices
8 ounces tostados

1 Combine the browned beef with the chopped onion, kidney beans, French dressing, water, chile and garlic. Simmer for 15 minutes. Season with salt to taste. Allow to cool for several hours, if possible, so that flavors blend. Skim off extra fat.

2 Fry tortillas in deep fat or oil. Fry on one side, turn, pinch up corners and hold with tongs to form cup shapes; or fry flat and crisp.

3 Combine the lettuce (both kinds) with the purple cabbage, scallions, tomatoes and 1½ cups of the cheese. Reheat the meat mixture.

4 Combine both mixtures and spoon generously into the crisp-fried tortilla cups. Garnish servings with avocado slices and remaining cheese. Stick a tostado into the top of each serving. Serve with a basket of crisp tostados.

Variations: *For a meatless and heartier vegetable combination similar to tostados popularly served in California, spread refried beans seasoned with garlic as in Tostados Compuestas (p. 68) on each fried tortilla. Place layers of sliced zucchini, radishes, mushrooms and roasted sunflower seeds on top of the beans. Then add the salad mixture as above. Instead of slicing the avocado, prepare guacamole and serve it over top of salads.*

AVOCADO FRUIT SALAD WITH POPPY-SEED DRESSING

4 servings

The surprising blend of flavors in this salad goes well with many Mexican main dishes. Though not traditional, this salad has become increasingly popular.

2 medium-size avocados
lemon or lime juice
2 medium-size oranges, or 1 large grapefruit
1 large Bermuda onion
8 large lettuce leaves
1 cup Poppy-Seed Dressing (recipe follows)

1 Peel avocados, halve, and remove pits. Dip avocados into an ascorbic-acid solution such as used for preserving fruits. Or sprinkle with fresh lemon or lime juice.

2 Peel oranges or grapefruit and onion. Cut oranges and onion into thin slices. For grapefruit, slice each section away from the membrane and remove. Separate onion slices into rings.

3 Place the lettuce leaves on salad plates. Arrange avocado slices with orange slices or grapefruit sections on lettuce. Top with onion rings. Drizzle with dressing. Serve immediately.

POPPY-SEED DRESSING

1½ cups dressing

1 cup oil
⅓ cup vinegar
¾ cup honey
1 teaspoon salt
1 teaspoon dry mustard
1 teaspoon celery seeds
1 small scallion
1 tablespoon poppy seeds

1 Place all ingredients in the container of an electric blender in the order listed and blend at high speed until scallion is puréed. (If no blender is available, mince the onion and mix the ingredients together with an electric mixer at high speed or a wire whisk.)

2 Store in a covered container in refrigerator for up to 2 weeks.

SOUTHWEST POTATO SALAD

8 servings

5 large red potatoes
3 eggs
6 slices of bacon, cut up
4 green onions, chopped
¼ pound butter (1 stick)
½ cup dry white wine
½ cup chicken stock
1 teaspoon seasoned salt
½ teaspoon freshly ground black pepper
¼ cup chopped green chile (optional)
¼ cup chopped pimiento
3 tablespoons chopped parsley
4 to 6 cherry tomatoes

1 Peel potatoes; cook until tender. Meanwhile, hard-cook eggs and fry bacon until crisp. Cook onion in the bacon drippings until onion is translucent. Drain off excess fat.

2 When potatoes are done, add the butter in chunks, then cube the potatoes, mixing in the butter so as to coat all the potato pieces evenly while hot.

3 Add remaining ingredients except 1 tablespoon parsley and cherry tomatoes. Mix well until blended. Serve while still warm, garnished with 1 tablespoon parsley and the cherry tomatoes.

EL PINTO SALAD

4 to 6 servings

Serve as the main dish for lunch or as a side dish for a hearty meal. Crusty squares of hot buttered corn bread are a tasty accompaniment.

2 cups cooked pinto beans, drained
4 hard-cooked eggs, chopped
1 cup ½-inch cubes of Monterey Jack cheese
¼ cup sweet onion rings
2 tablespoons oil
1 tablespoon vinegar
1 tablespoon red chile sauce
1 teaspoon prepared mustard
¼ teaspoon each of salt and pepper
¼ cup bacon bits (optional)
4 to 6 lettuce leaves
4 to 6 parsley sprigs

1 Mix together the beans, eggs, cheese and onion rings. Chill.

2 Combine remaining ingredients and pour over the bean mixture. Mix well. Sprinkle with crisp bacon bits if desired.

3 Serve on lettuce cups, garnished with fresh parsley.

CORN RELISH SALAD

6 servings

1½ cups cooked corn kernels, or 12 ounces canned whole-kernel corn, drained
¼ cup well-drained sweet pickle relish
½ cup sliced pitted black olives
½ cup sliced celery
1 teaspoon salt
2 tablespoons sugar
2 tablespoons wine vinegar
6 tablespoons salad oil
2 quarts shredded salad greens

1 Combine corn, pickle relish, olives and celery. Dissolve salt and sugar in vinegar in a small jar with a tight-fitting lid. Add the salad oil; cover and shake.

2 Pour over the corn mixture. Chill for several hours, stirring occasionally. Add salad greens; toss lightly to mix.

Note: *For a relish or hors d'oeuvre serve the pickled corn in a deep bowl encircled with lettuce leaves. For a very large party, you will want to double or triple the relish part of the recipe.*

EGG DISHES

Eggs are particularly exciting when combined with chiles, cheese, tomatoes or tortillas and flavored with traditional Tex-Mex seasonings. The following specialties are excellent served most any time of day, from dawn to midnight. Somehow, either the spicy sauce or chile is very sumptuous when served with the tender, mild egg.

HUEVOS RANCHEROS
Ranch Eggs

4 servings

This variation of heuvos rancheros is my favorite, discovered in a sunny little Mexican border restaurant. For cheers, first serve Bloody Marias (p. 36). Serve with additional warm flour or corn tortillas, sweet butter and honey.

SAUCE

2 tablespoons bacon drippings or melted butter
2 medium-size onions, thinly sliced and separated into rings
4 medium-size tomatoes, sliced into thin wedges
8 to 12 green chiles, parched (p. 21), peeled and chopped
¼ cup flour
1 garlic clove, finely minced
1 teaspoon salt
dash of ground comino
3 cups chicken stock

1 Melt butter in a frypan over medium heat. Add the onions, tomatoes and chiles, and cook until onions are translucent. Add the flour and stir and cook until well blended.

2 Add garlic and seasonings and the stock (use less stock if a very thick sauce is desired). Cook until the sauce becomes smooth and continue to cook for about 15 minutes to blend the flavors. Meanwhile prepare rest of recipe:

8 flour tortillas (corn tortillas can be substituted)
8 eggs
1 cup grated Monterey Jack or sharp Cheddar cheese
2 cups coarsely shredded romaine lettuce
1 medium-size tomato, cut into 12 thin wedges, or 12 cherry tomatoes

3 Preheat oven to 350°F. Wrap tortillas in foil, allowing one or two per person. Place foil packages on plates to be used for serving (Mexican pottery is extra nice) and set in preheated oven. (At the same time, you can also warm the extra tortillas you are serving as a bread.)

4 Just before serving, poach the eggs. To serve, unwrap the warm tortillas and place them in the center of the warmed plates. Top each tortilla with 1 or 2 poached eggs.

5 Spoon on sauce, dividing it equally among the 4 servings. Top each serving with ¼ cup grated cheese. Return to the oven until cheese melts, 2 to 5 minutes.

6 Encircle each plate with shredded lettuce. Place 3 tomato wedges or cherry tomatoes on top of the lettuce. Serve immediately.

Maximum Recommended Freezer Storage: *3 months for the sauce*

CALIFORNIA-STYLE HUEVOS RANCHEROS

4 servings

This colorful version of huevos rancheros is particularly good for entertaining. Serve fresh fruit, warm wheat-flour tortillas, sweet butter, honey and coffee for a great brunch.

1 tablespoon olive oil
½ medium-size onion, chopped
¾ cup tomato juice, or ½ cup tomato sauce thinned with 2 tablespoons water
1 small garlic clove, minced
3 whole chiles, parched (p. 21), peeled and chopped, or 4 ounces canned whole green chiles, chopped
¾ teaspoon ground comino
¼ teaspoon ground Mexican orégano
½ teaspoon salt
4 corn tortillas
4 to 8 eggs
2 avocados, peeled and thinly sliced lengthwise
½ cup grated Monterey Jack or Cheddar cheese
4 lettuce leaves, coarsely chopped

1 In a medium-size saucepan, heat the oil, add the chopped onion, and fry over medium heat until onion is translucent. Add tomato juice, garlic, chiles, herbs and salt. Reduce heat to simmer for about 10 minutes. Sauce can be made a day or hours ahead of time and left at this point.

2 Preheat oven to 350°F. Warm the tortillas by wrapping in foil and placing on the 4 serving plates (Mexican pottery if possible) in the warm oven. At the same time, warm the extra tortillas you are serving as bread.

3 Poach the eggs, using an egg poacher or a frying pan of hot water with 2 tablespoons vinegar and 1 teaspoon salt added. First break an egg into a cup, then stir the water in the frying pan vigorously in a circular motion. As you stir, slide the egg from the cup into the water. Cover the pan when all eggs have been added.

4 To assemble the dish, place a tortilla on a plate. Top with a circle of avocado slices, then arrange a drained poached egg (or 2 eggs) on top, spoon sauce over, and sprinkle with cheese. Place in the oven until cheese melts. Add the lettuce garnish after the cheese has melted.

Variation: *Instead of the tortillas, rinse large "cupped" iceberg lettuce leaves and serve the eggs topped with sauce in the lettuce leaves.*

Not Recommended for Freezing

BEEFY HUEVOS RANCHEROS

For a variation of Huevos Rancheros (p. 78), lightly fry ½ pound ground lean beef, drain, then follow the rest of the directions for the sauce. Instead of adding chicken stock, add 2 cups beef stock and cook until flavors blend and sauce is as thick as desired. This generally is thicker than the chicken-based sauce. However, if a thinner sauce is preferred, use more beef stock.

Maximum Recommended Freezer Storage: *3 months*

CHILE POACHED EGGS   4 servings

Another variation of huevos rancheros; Green Chile Stew (p. 64) works well as the sauce for this dish.

4 to 6 green chiles, chopped
1 onion, chopped
1 fresh tomato, peeled and chopped
2½ cups beef stock
1 garlic clove, minced
1 pinch of ground Mexican orégano
½ teaspoon salt
4 large wheat-flour tortillas
8 eggs
1 cup coarsely chopped lettuce (optional)

1 (Omit this sauce preparation if using prepared chile stew.) Simmer together the chiles, onion, tomato, beef stock, garlic, orégano and salt in a frying pan. When onion is tender, and liquid has thickened to a soup consistency, sauce is ready.

2 Place the tortillas on 4 plates, cover with foil, and heat in a 350°F. oven. Also, heat additional tortillas for serving as a bread.

3 Break an egg into a cup. Stir a small portion of the sauce in a circular motion and then slip the egg into the sauce where you've stirred it. Repeat with the rest of the eggs. Cover the pan and cook until the eggs are done as desired.

4 Place 2 eggs on each tortilla and cover with the sauce. Garnish with coarsely chopped lettuce if desired.

Maximum Recommmended Freezer Storage: *8 months for the sauce*

SANTA FE OMELET

4 servings

Create this special dish for any meal—brunch, lunch or supper. This easy-to-prepare, tasty omelet is great combined with fresh fruits and Navajo Fry Bread (p. 54) oozing with homemade jam and melting butter.

butter
8 eggs
¼ cup light cream or beer
½ teaspoon salt
freshly ground black pepper
2 cups cheese sauce (follows)
4 to 6 green chiles, parched (p. 21) and peeled, or 4 ounces canned whole green chiles

1 Prepare cheese sauce.
2 Lightly butter a frypan or omelet pan and heat. Beat the eggs with a whisk or fork until foamy. Add the cream and seasonings. Mix well.
3 Pour the egg mixture into the skillet and cook until the eggs are firm.
4 To serve, place the green chiles evenly over half of the omelet. Fold the other half over and remove to a serving platter. Drizzle with the cheese sauce. Garnish as desired.

CHEESE SAUCE

2 cups

2 tablespoons butter
2 tablespoons flour
2 cups milk
½ cup cubed Monterey Jack cheese
¾ teaspoon salt
½ teaspoon dry mustard
dash Worcestershire sauce

1 Melt butter in a medium-size saucepan. Stir in flour and heat until the flour slightly browns. Then slowly stir in the milk, making sure no lumps form.
2 Cook and stir until the sauce is smooth and begins to thicken. Add the cheese and seasonings and stir to uniformly blend. Taste and adjust seasonings. After the cheese is melted, cook for about 15 minutes to develop the seasonings.

Variation: *For a less rich dish, cube enough Monterey Jack cheese to make ½ cup or more and sprinkle over the top of the omelet as it cooks. Omit cheese sauce.*

Not Recommended for Freezing

SPANISH OMELET

2 to 3 servings

3 large tomatoes, cubed
1 onion, chopped
1 garlic clove, minced
2 celery ribs, finely sliced
½ teaspoon salt
6 tablespoons butter
½ cup cooked peas
3 green chiles, parched (p. 21), peeled and sliced into rings
6 eggs
¼ cup water or beer
½ teaspoon salt
generous dash of freshly ground black pepper

1 Using a large frying pan, cook the tomatoes, onion, garlic, celery and salt in 3 tablespoons butter until soft. Add the cooked peas and green chiles after the other vegetables are soft, about 5 minutes.

2 Remove the vegetables from the pan and add remaining butter. While it's melting, beat the eggs with the water or beer, salt and pepper. Add all at once to the frying pan and cook until the eggs set.

3 Slide onto a platter and spoon most of the vegetables over, then fold omelet and drizzle remaining vegetables over the top. Serve immediately.

Not Recommended for Freezing

CHILE PIE
Green Chile-Crusted Cheese Custard

6 to 8 servings

A simple, quick-to-prepare dish, good any time of day, even as an hors d'oeuvre when cut into small squares.

1 teaspoon butter
8 whole green chiles, parched (p. 21) and peeled, or 8 ounces canned green chiles
¼ pound Monterey Jack cheese, grated
5 eggs, slightly beaten
½ cup cream
¾ teaspoon salt
freshly ground black pepper

1 Preheat oven to 350°F. (325°F. if using a glass baking dish).

2 Butter a 10-inch pie pan. Cut chiles open and use them to line pie pan, allowing tops of chiles to come to top edge of pan.

3 Spread cheese evenly over chiles.

4 Beat eggs until frothy, using a fork or whisk; add cream and seasonings and beat together. Pour into the chile-lined pan.

5 Bake for 30 minutes, or until eggs are set and top is light golden brown.

Not Recommended for Freezing

CHORIZO EGGS

4 servings

4 whole Chorizos (p. 130), skinned and finely chopped, or 1 pound bulk chorizo
8 eggs
¼ cup beer or milk
½ teaspoon salt
¼ teaspoon crushed comino
4 lettuce leaves, shredded
4 slices of tomato
8 pitted ripe olives, sliced
¼ cup sour cream (optional)
2 tablespoons chopped sweet purple onion (optional)

1 Over medium high heat, cook the chorizo until it is slightly browned. Drain grease.

2 Mix the eggs, beer or milk, salt and comino together, using a fork to blend them until frothy.

3 Reduce heat to medium low, add the eggs to the chorizo and cook, stirring frequently, until the eggs are set but soft.

4 Serve on plates garnished with shredded lettuce, topped with tomato wedges and sprinkled with olive slices. Top each serving with sour cream and onion, if desired. This garnish is especially nice for brunch or luncheon serving.

Not Recommended for Freezing

TEX-MEX
SPECIALTIES

From enchiladas to chile con carne...there are many unique flavors, textures and serving combinations that are traditionally Tex-Mex. As you will see while reading the following recipes, ingredients such as blue cornmeal, sour cream and olives are not used in the same way as they are in Mexican cooking. Chile con carne is not Mexican in the least, but a thick chile-flavored stew from Texas that has as many variations as there are chile cooks. The best-known specialties out of the Southwest are probably tacos and chile—yet within the region, enchiladas, rellenos, burritos and tamales are the most popular. New favorites are flautas and chimichangos; however, not too many restaurants feature them.

ENCHILADAS

Enchiladas are one of the most popular Tex-Mex and Mexican foods. Though not quite as versatile as tacos, they can also be prepared in numerous ways. Rolled enchiladas are the most popular. They are made by frying a corn tortilla, stuffing it with grated sharp cheese such as Monterey Jack, adding chopped onion if desired, and heating it in red or green chile sauce until bubbly.

Shredded pork, fried ground beef, chorizo or shredded chicken can be added to the chile sauce. Authentic, southern Rio Grande enchiladas are served open-faced without rolling. The filling is layered between the tortillas, then topped generously with more sauce and heated. They are often served garnished with a fried egg or sour cream and olives.

Enchiladas can be made a day or two ahead. If you're cooking for a crowd, prepare them rolled up and place in an earthenware casserole. Prepare the sauce in advance too. At serving time pour the sauce over the enchiladas and heat until bubbly. Serve garnished with shredded lettuce and cherry tomatoes.

ENCHILADAS
Tortillas with Chiles and Cheese   2 servings

6 yellow or blue corn tortillas
oil
3 cups Red Chile Sauce (p. 44)
1 cup grated Monterey Jack or sharp cheese
1 onion, chopped (may be cooked into the sauce)
6 to 8 lettuce leaves, chopped
4 cherry tomatoes, halved
2 eggs, lightly fried (optional)

1 Lightly fry the tortillas in shallow oil over medium heat, then drain on absorbent toweling. Or for fewer calories, place the tortillas on dinner plates, cover with foil, and place in a moderate oven until they are warm and soft.

2 For *rolled enchiladas*, dip a lightly fried tortilla into the sauce and place a strip of grated cheese and chopped onion down the center. Add a strip of cooked meat, if desired. Roll and top with more sauce and cheese. Continue until all are rolled.

3 For individual servings, place 2 or 3 enchiladas on each plate. To serve a crowd, place the rolled enchiladas in a buttered, large shallow baking dish.

Wait to cover them with sauce and cheese until just before heating to serve. Cook only until the sauce begins to bubble and the cheese melts. Add lettuce and tomatoes around the edges before serving.

4 For *flat enchiladas,* place a little sauce on a plate, then top with a tortilla, followed by cheese, onion and more sauce. Repeat twice more. Top each enchilada with more sauce and cheese. Heat in a moderate oven until the cheese melts. Top with an egg, if desired, and garnish around the edges with chopped lettuce and tomatoes.

Freezing Hints: *Rolled enchiladas can be frozen in a casserole, but freeze the sauce separately.*

Maximum Recommended Freezer Storage: *3 months*

CHORIZO ENCHILADAS
Mexican Sausages with Tortillas
6 servings

These extra special enchiladas are great when served with a dollop of sour cream and guacamole.

2 pounds Chorizo, either bulk or links (p. 130)
4 cups Red Chile Sauce (p. 44)
12 corn tortillas
cooking oil
3 cups grated Longhorn cheese
1 pint sour cream
2 cups shredded lettuce
1 recipe Guacamole (p. 26)
ripe olives

1 Remove the chorizo from the casings, if using links, and crumble. Place in a heavy frying pan and cook, stirring often to keep the sausage crumbly. Drain well.

2 Add the red chile sauce to the drained meat in the frying pan and cook and stir to blend flavors, about 15 minutes. Place 6 earthenware plates in an oven set at 350°F. to warm.

3 Lightly fry the tortillas and drain them between layers of paper towels.

4 Assemble the enchiladas: place a spoon of meat sauce on each plate, then top with a tortilla, more sauce, a sprinkle of cheese, and repeat.

5 Heat in the oven to melt the cheese, for 3 to 5 minutes. To serve, top with sour cream and encircle enchiladas with lettuce and guacamole; garnish with ripe olives.

GREEN CHILE ENCHILADAS 4 servings

These are popular with every Gringo or Tex-Mex friend to whom I have served them. Because they are a meal in themselves, I only serve guacamole before and sopaipillas and honey alongside.

2 tablespoons flour
¼ cup water
4 cups chicken stock
1 cup chopped cooked chicken
½ to 1 cup green chiles, parched (p. 21), peeled and chopped
1 teaspoon ground comino
salt
1 garlic clove, crushed
12 tortillas (blue corn tortillas are best)
cooking oil
1½ cups grated Monterey Jack or Cheddar cheese, or more
1 medium-size onion, chopped
2 cups sour cream
4 eggs, lightly fried (optional)
romaine or head lettuce, coarsely chopped
2 fresh tomatoes, cut into wedges (optional)

1 Mix the flour with the water to make a smooth paste, then combine with the stock and blend well in a 2-quart saucepan. Cook until slightly thickened. Add chicken and green chiles. Season with comino, salt to taste and garlic, and simmer together for about 15 minutes. Add more flour mixed with water if a thicker sauce is desired.

2 Meanwhile, lightly fry the tortillas in about 1 inch of hot oil in a frying pan. Warm 4 plates in the oven.

3 Combine 1 cup of the grated cheese with the chopped onion and sour cream.

4 Prepare the enchiladas by placing a spoonful of sauce on each warm plate. Lay a tortilla on top, then spoon on more sauce to cover the tortilla and add a spoonful of the sour-cream mixture. Continue until each plate has 3 tortillas and all the sauce is used. Top each with a generous dollop of the sour-cream mixture and sprinkle with remaining grated cheese.

5 Place in a 400°F. oven to melt the cheese. When the cheese is melted, place a fried egg on each stack of tortillas if you wish. Top and encircle each enchilada with chopped lettuce and tomato wedges.

Variations: *Beef can be substituted for the chicken; use beef stock instead of chicken stock. Pork also can be used. Any type of leftover meat is good used in the sauce.*

If preferred, the enchiladas may be served rolled instead of flat. To do this, dip the tortillas into the sauce, add a spoonful of the onion-cheese mixture, and roll. Place rolled enchiladas in a buttered casserole and top with remaining sauce. Sprinkle additional grated cheese on top of enchiladas, and heat. If preparing in advance, wait to add the sauce until just before heating.

Freezing Hints: *Only the sauce freezes well. If unexpected crises occur, a casserole of rolled enchiladas could be frozen, but they do suffer somewhat. Freeze the sauce separately.*

Maximum Recommended Freezer Storage: *3 months*

★ ★

BAKED ENCHILADAS CON POLLO
Chicken Enchiladas
4 to 6 servings

1 tablespoon flour
1 cup chicken stock
1 pint whipping cream
2 scallions with tops, chopped
1 teaspoon salt
freshly ground black pepper
1 pint sour cream
12 corn tortillas
3 cups cooked breast of chicken
2 whole canned pimientos, cut into long strips
½ pound sharp Cheddar cheese, grated
Green Chile Sauce or Salsa (p. 42)
lettuce, coarsely chopped

1 Preheat oven to 350°F. Mix flour with stock and heat until slightly thickened. Add the whipping cream, scallions, salt and pepper. Bring to a boil. Stir in the sour cream until well mixed.

2 Dip each tortilla into the cream mixture, then arrange chicken and pimiento down the center of each; roll up.

3 Place rolled enchiladas in a greased flat baking dish. Pour remaining cream mixture over them and bake for 30 minutes.

4 Sprinkle cheese over the enchiladas and heat until melted. Serve with green chile sauce or salsa. Encircle the dish with coarsely chopped lettuce.

Variations: *Because this dish is so rich you may prefer to use buttermilk in place of the sour cream and light cream instead of whipping cream.*

Freezing Hints: *Place crisscrossed pieces of foil inside the casserole dish in which you wish to serve. Spoon in the filling, then freeze until solid, about 2 days. Remove from casserole dish and package for freezing. To serve, thaw slightly, remove foil and replace in casserole dish. Bake for 45 minutes, or until bubbly and hot.*

Maximum Recommended Freezer Storage: *3 months*

CRAB-FILLED GREEN CHILE ENCHILADAS

4 servings

A California invention, rarely seen on menus. I first savored them in Sacramento a few years ago and developed this recipe, which has become a favorite.

1 recipe Green Chile Sauce (p. 42)
8 corn tortillas
cooking oil
1 cup cooked crab meat, fresh, frozen or canned
6 scallions, tops included, chopped
2 cups grated Monterey Jack cheese
2 cups sour cream
½ cup large pimiento-stuffed green olives, halved
romaine lettuce, coarsely chopped

1 Prepare the sauce and keep warm. Heat 4 pottery plates in a 350°F. oven. Lightly fry the tortillas in about 1 inch of cooking oil in a frying pan. Drain well on paper towels.

2 Prepare the enchiladas: place a spoonful of the green sauce on each warm plate. Top with a tortilla, more sauce, one quarter of the crab, chopped scallion and cheese, then another tortilla. Repeat for the other portions.

3 Heat in the warm oven until the cheese melts. Top each with ½ cup sour cream and one quarter of the olives.

4 Encircle with chopped lettuce and serve immediately.

Variation: *If preferred, these can be prepared as rolled enchiladas; use the cheese, onion and crab for the filling.*

Not Recommended for Freezing

TACOS

The most popular Mexican snack is the taco. The fillings can vary from substantial meaty mixtures to lighter, salad-type stuffings. Tacos can be tailored to most any appetite and can be served most any time of day. They don't have to be just a snack either; they can serve as the main entrée when prepared with a hearty filling and served with such side dishes as frijoles refritos, refried pinto beans and/or Mexican rice or posole.

The key ingredient for a taco is a crisp-fried corn tortilla, folded into a U shape as it is fried. Taco fryers can be convenient, as they hold the tortillas in the desired shape while frying. For extra convenience, prefried and shaped taco shells are available. The shells are traditionally filled with a seasoned meat or bean filling, layered with shredded lettuce, chopped onion, tomato and grated cheese, and sauced with a red or green chile sauce to taste.

Variations for tacos are endless. A few favorites are beef, fried chopped beef or shredded roast beef; pork or chile pork (carne adobada); sausage (Mexican chorizo is super); chicken, turkey, ham, chile con carne, refried beans or even meat loaf.

Garnishes in addition to the traditional ones can be sour cream, guacamole or chile con queso laced with chopped olives, thinly sliced radish rounds or circles of fresh green pepper. Taco sauce or salsa made of tomatoes, onion, chiles, garlic and spices creates the Mexican flavor.

Another plus is that tacos can be a great way to use leftover meats and salad stuffs. Most any type of meat is usable. Use your imagination and your family's or guests' tastes as a guide. Taco fillings can be frozen for 3 months, if there is any left over, the taco shells can be frozen for 2 months.

Tacos are festive for parties, especially for casual do-it-yourself buffets, because they are so easily eaten—just like a sandwich from a napkin or saucer. That makes forks optional and simplifies things for the host or hostess. For a buffet, try creating a taco bar, placing bowls of fillings, toppers and sauces along with favorite beverages.

BEEF TACOS

12 tacos

12 corn tortillas
cooking oil
1 pound ground beef
2 tablespoons ground mild red chile
½ teaspoon ground Mexican orégano
½ teaspoon ground comino
1 garlic clove, crushed
½ teaspoon salt
1 small onion, chopped
1 fresh tomato, coarsely chopped
2 cups shredded lettuce
1½ to 2 cups grated sharp cheese
any Salsa (p. 42)

1 Fry tortillas on both sides in ½ inch or more of hot oil. Fry each tortilla on one side until slightly crisp but still pliable, then turn and fold in half. Allow one side to become crisp, then turn and fry the last side. You may want to fry several taco shells at a time and freeze the extras.

2 Crumble beef into a skillet, add chile, orégano, comino, garlic and salt, and fry until browned and thoroughly cooked. Drain off excess fat.

3 Place the meat in the taco shells. Add the chopped onion, tomato, lettuce and cheese in layers. Heat briefly in a 450°F. oven to melt cheese. Serve nested with extra lettuce and a side dish of salsa.

Variations: *Leftover shredded roast beef may be used instead of ground beef. Refried beans or guacamole may be used instead of the beef or in addition. For extra flavor or quantity, add 2 cups cooked or canned pinto beans to the beef.*

Freezing Hints: *Freeze taco shells and filling separately. Keep the shells from breaking by stuffing a wadded paper towel or foil inside each shell. Freeze them in a rigid container.*

Maximum Recommended Freezer Storage: *1 year for taco shells, 3 months for beef filling*

CHICKEN TACOS

My favorite tacos! Try these as a snack or light luncheon, or as a side dish for a combination Mexican plate.

Follow the recipe for Beef Tacos (preceding recipe). Use blue-corn tortillas if available, and instead of fried spiced beef use 2 cups boned cooked chicken. Do not season the chicken with anything except a bit of salt. Place the chicken in the fried shells and top with the salad mixture which has been mixed together and seasoned with a crushed garlic clove. Top generously with grated Monterey Jack cheese. Warm until the cheese melts and serve immediately with a side dish of freshly made Salsa (p. 42).

Freezing Hints: *Follow directions for Beef Tacos.*

PORK TACOS

10 tacos

A great use for leftover pork.

2 tablespoons lard or bacon drippings
2 cups shredded cooked pork
1 small onion, sliced and separated into rings
1 medium-size garlic clove, minced
salt
6 lettuce leaves, chopped
1 medium-size tomato, chopped
1 cup grated Monterey Jack cheese
10 corn tortillas
cooking oil
any Salsa (p. 42)

1 Melt lard or drippings in a skillet. Add pork and cook, stirring occasionally, until lightly browned. Add onion and garlic and cook until onion is soft. Simmer, uncovered, for 5 minutes. Season with salt to taste. Meanwhile prepare lettuce, tomato and cheese. Fry tortillas and fold to make taco shells (see Beef Tacos, p. 92, for directions).

2 Spoon 2 to 3 tablespoons meat filling in each taco shell. Add rest of ingredients in layers.

3 Heat in a 400°F. oven until the cheese melts, about 5 minutes.

CARNE ASADA SOFT TACOS

12 tacos

1 pound beef filet
12 corn tortillas, warmed in foil or briefly in oven
1 medium-size sweet onion, finely chopped
2 medium-size tomatoes, finely chopped
2 cups shredded lettuce
fresh Salsa (p. 42)

1 Charcoal-broil the filet. As it is getting done, warm the tortillas on dinner plates in a 350°F. oven.

2 Thinly slice the beef and place in a Mexican pottery bowl. Place the onion, tomatoes, lettuce and salsa in similar bowls. Place the tortillas in a napkin-lined basket.

3 Assemble the tacos by placing a layer of meat in a tortilla, then layers of onion, tomatoes, lettuce and salsa.

CHORIZO TACOS

12 tacos

Chorizo is in many ways an easier filling than other meats such as ground beef since the sausage is already so well seasoned.

12 corn tortillas, either yellow or blue
cooking oil
1 pound chorizo sausage, links or bulk
1 recipe Guacamole (p. 26)
1 pint sour cream
2 cups shredded iceberg lettuce
1 cup grated Monterey Jack cheese
36 stuffed green olives
fresh Salsa (p. 42)

1 Fry tortillas and fold to make taco shells (see Beef Tacos, p. 92, for directions).

2 If sausage is in links, remove from casings. Crumble the sausage into a large heavy skillet. Heat to medium and stir to continue crumbling. Fry until well done, about 20 minutes, then drain well.

3 Place a layer of the meat in the taco shells, then layers of guacamole, sour cream, lettuce and cheese. Garnish with the olives. If desired, serve with taco sauce or fresh salsa.

AMY'S TACOS

4 tacos

Children of any age are sure to agree with my daughter Amy who loves these tacos served with coleslaw.

1 tablespoon ground mild red chile
½ teaspoon each of ground Mexican orégano and comino
1 garlic clove, crushed
salt
½ pound ground beef
1 medium-size tomato, chopped
2 tablespoons chopped onion
¼ cup shredded Monterey Jack or Cheddar cheese
4 taco shells
any Salsa (p. 42)

1 Mix the chile, orégano, comino, garlic and ½ teaspoon salt together. Add the seasoning mix to the ground beef. Cook in a skillet until done. Taste and add more seasoning, perhaps more salt also. Drain off excess fat.

2 Prepare the rest of the filling ingredients. Add to taco shells in order listed, sprinkling with salt as you layer in the ingredients.

3 Place 2 tacos on each heatproof plate and heat in a 400°F. oven until cheese bubbles, about 5 minutes. Serve with salsa.

Freezing Hints: *Follow directions for Beef Tacos (p. 92).*

ENVUELTOS
Chicken-Stuffed Soft Tortillas

3 to 6 servings

6 blue, yellow, or white corn tortillas
1 cup shredded cooked chicken breast
salt
pinch of minced fresh cilantro
1 garlic clove, crushed
3 green chiles, parched (p. 21), peeled and chopped, or 4 ounces canned chopped green chiles
½ cup sour cream
1 teaspoon jalapeño pickle juice, or more
1 cup (about) shredded lettuce
1 large fresh tomato, cut into wedges
1 avocado, peeled, pitted and cut into long slivers

1 Wrap the tortillas in foil and heat on 3 or 6 plates (3 plates if serving as a main course, 6 plates if serving as a snack). Meanwhile, prepare the chicken and season with salt; mix in cilantro and garlic.

2 When tortillas are heated through, about 15 minutes, place one or more on each plate. Spoon one-sixth of the chicken down the center of each tortilla. Divide the chopped green chile into 6 portions and place on top of the chicken. Roll each tortilla around the stuffing and place it seam side down to hold it together. Place each plateful in the oven to heat a few minutes.

3 Combine the sour cream with the jalapeño juice, making it as hot as desired by adding juice to taste. Place some sour cream on top of each stuffed tortilla.

4 Encircle tortillas with lettuce, tomato and avocado slivers.

Variation: *If some of those eating prefer milder seasoning, do not add the jalapeño juice to the sour cream; instead serve a spicy salsa alongside.*

Not Recommended for Freezing

FLAUTAS
Fried Filled Tortillas

4 to 6 servings

These fried rolled tacos look like flutes, the origin of their name.

12 corn tortillas
about 1½ cups cooked meat filling such as beef, pork or chicken (pp. 92 and 93)
lard
shredded lettuce
Salsa (p. 42)
sour cream

1 Wrap the tortillas in foil and heat in an oven for about 15 minutes to soften; or place each one briefly on a hot griddle.

2 Using 2 spoons, place a narrow pile of filling along the center of each tortilla, working on only one at a time. Roll and secure with a toothpick.

3 While rolling the flautas, heat about ¼ inch of lard to medium heat in a large heavy skillet. Fry the flautas, turning to brown evenly. Drain on paper towels. Serve garnished with lettuce, salsa and sour cream to taste.

Variation: *Serve plain with a bowl of salsa for guests to dip their own.*

Maximum Recommended Freezer Storage: *3 months*

CHIMICHANGOS
Wheat-Flour Tortillas Filled with Beef and Deep-Fried

6 servings

In the cities nearest the Mexican border, particularly in El Paso and Tucson, a new favorite has become established as one of the specialties. In restaurants featuring chimichangos, the managements seem to agree that they have become their most requested dish. Since the recipe is kept closely guarded, I found I had to develop this recipe myself after many samplings and conversations with the secretive restaurateurs.

2 pounds lean stewing beef, coarsely chopped
2 medium-size potatoes, diced in small squares
6 medium-size hot green chiles, parched (p. 21), peeled and chopped
1 large onion, chopped
2 garlic cloves, minced
1 teaspoon ground Mexican orégano
2 teaspoons salt
water
lard
12 wheat-flour tortillas
2 cups shredded lettuce
12 cherry tomatoes
1 pint sour cream
Guacamole (p. 26)

1 Place the beef, potatoes, green chiles, onion, garlic, Mexican orégano and salt in a saucepan and barely cover with water. Cover and simmer for at least 1 hour, or until all ingredients are well done and very soft.

2 Taste and adjust seasoning. If mixture is still soupy, remove lid and cook until the "stew" becomes quite thick.

3 Heat about 2 inches of lard in a heavy skillet until quite hot.

4 Divide the filling among the tortillas, placing about 2 heaping tablespoons in the center of each. Fold one side of the tortilla over the filling, then fold over each of the adjacent two sides and finally fold the fourth side over the top.

5 Meanwhile warm 6 plates in a 300°F. oven. Carefully fry the filled tortillas until golden, turning to assure even browning. Drain and place two on each warm plate in the oven.

6 Serve encircled with the lettuce and cherry tomatoes. Spoon sour cream, then guacamole over the tops.

Maximum Recommended Freezer Storage: *3 months*

NEW MEXICO CHALUPAS
Cornmeal Crust Topped with Meat Salad — 4 to 6 servings

Little boats filled with an assortment of mouth-watering Mexican treats characterize this one-dish meal. Chalupas means "little boats," but the word on a Mexican menu can have many interpretations, from hors d'oeuvre to full-size servings.

¼ cup lard, softened
1½ cups instant masa harina (corn tortilla flour sold in Mexican specialty markets outside the Southwest)
salt
¾ cup water, approximately
cooking oil
Salsa (p. 42)
Guacamole (p. 26)
3 cups cooked chicken, turkey or beef, seasoned to taste
pepper
2 cups refried beans
1 garlic clove, crushed
4 ounces Monterey Jack cheese, shredded
sour cream
1 cup stuffed Spanish olives
lettuce, coarsely shredded
fresh cilantro or Chinese parsley, if available

1 Prepare the masa dough: fluff the lard by beating with a wooden spoon or in the small bowl of an electric mixer on medium-high speed. Stir in the masa harina, or turn the mixer to low and add the masa and ½ teaspoon salt.

2 Add the water a little at a time, continuing to beat. If using the mixer, switch to medium speed and beat until the dough becomes quite fluffy.

3 Divide the dough into 4 large or 6 medium-size balls and roll out between sheets of wax paper to about ¼-inch thickness. The dough can be prepared ahead and allowed to set overnight or it can be frozen for at least 3 months if sealed well.

4 Next, prepare the layers of filling which are the salsa, guacamole and meat. Shred or chop the meat, then season with salt and pepper to taste. Heat the refried beans with the garlic and cheese over medium-low heat, stirring frequently.

5 Bake masa crust on a preheated, lightly oiled griddle or large frying pan heated to 350°F. or medium. Fry for about 3 minutes on each side, or until light brown.

6 Prepare the chalupas for everyone, or place all ingredients in separate bowls on the table and let each guest assemble his or her own.

7 To prepare, place a layer of guacamole on the fried crust, then some of the cheesy beans, spread out the beans, leaving about ½-inch margin of guacamole showing around the edges. Next, add the layer of meat, leaving a margin of beans about ½ inch all around. Top with salsa, sour cream and Spanish olives. Garnish edges with lettuce and cilantro.

Maximum Recommended Freezer Storage: *2 months for uncooked masa crusts; 6 months for cooked masa crusts*

BURRITOS A LA BUTEL
Wheat Tortillas Wrapped Around Refried Beans 6 servings

Burritos are delicious when made well, but disappointing when poorly made or served sauceless. I developed this sauce after tasting it numerous times in a Juarez, Mexico, restaurant. The sauce freezes very well; it is good also for huevos rancheros; however, Red or Green Chile Sauce (p. 44 and 42) can be substituted.

6 wheat-flour tortillas
2 cups cooked pinto beans, drained
1 teaspoon bacon drippings or butter
dash of salt
1 garlic clove, crushed
2 scallions, finely chopped
¾ cup grated Monterey Jack cheese
romaine lettuce or any green leafy lettuce, coarsely chopped

1 If tortillas are not freshly made, cover them with aluminum foil and heat on the dinner plates in a 300°F. oven. Heat the plates in any case.

2 Cook the beans in the drippings, mashing the beans to a pulp; season to taste with salt and add the garlic.

3 Spoon the hot bean mixture down the center of the warm tortillas. Top with chopped scallions and cheese. Roll. Heat in the oven until the cheese melts. Nest chopped lettuce around the warm burritos. Serve with a generous supply of Burrito Sauce (recipe follows).

Variation: *Chile con carne made from beef or pork can be used as filling in the burritos if desired.*

BURRITO SAUCE

2 cups sauce

1 tablespoon butter, melted
1 medium-size onion, thinly sliced and separated into rings
2 medium-size tomatoes, chopped, or 1 cup tomato sauce
4 to 6 green chiles, parched (p. 21), peeled and chopped, or 6 to 8 banana peppers sliced into rings
1 tablespoon flour
1 garlic clove, crushed
½ teaspoon salt
1½ cups chicken stock

1 Melt butter in a frypan. Add the onion, tomatoes and chiles; cook until the onion is translucent. Add the flour and stir and cook until well blended.

2 Add pepper rings, garlic, salt and stock. Cook until the sauce becomes smooth, then continue to cook for about 15 minutes to blend the flavors. Serve as a sauce with burritos, or use as a sauce over poached eggs atop tortillas to create huevos rancheros.

Freezing Hints: *The tortillas, bean filling and sauce freeze best separately. To freeze, package in sealed rigid cartons. If some burritos are left, they can be frozen individually wrapped if they have not been sauced.*

Maximum Recommended Freezer Storage: *3 months*

CHILE CON CARNE

Chile is as American as hot dogs and hamburgers. Mexicans and Spanish Americans rarely eat, or have even heard of, the type of chile we generally think of as chile con carne. Here are some very special chile recipes, including my favorites. Time usually dictates which I prepare. Often I make a double or triple recipe, freezing the extra in various-size cartons for convenience.

Favorite toppings that I like to serve are sour cream topped with chopped green or purple onion and coarsely grated cheese or whipped sour cream with a touch of fresh lime juice.

PECOS RIVER BOWL OF RED
12 servings

No collection of Tex-Mex recipes would be complete without this. Serve piping hot with crackers, tamales, wedges of cheese, dill-pickle strips and cold beer.

2 tablespoons lard, butter or bacon drippings
1 large onion, chopped
3 pounds lean beef, ground or coarsely chopped
3 garlic cloves, chopped
3 tablespoons ground hot red chile, or more
2 tablespoons ground mild red chile, or more
1 tablespoon ground comino
2 teaspoons salt
1 tablespoon paprika
3 cups water

1 Sauté the onion in the melted fat.

2 Mix the beef with the garlic, chile and comino.

3 Add the meat and seasonings to the onion; cook for 15 minutes, or until the meat is browned.

4 Add the remaining ingredients; stir well. Simmer over low heat for 1 to 2 hours, until the meat is very tender and the flavors are well blended. Taste and add more seasoning if desired.

5 If time allows, cool, then chill in the refrigerator. Peel off the fat. If time will not allow chilling, drain or skim off fat.

Variations: *If desired, serve with a dollop of sour cream, chopped scallion or sweet onion and coarsely grated Monterey Jack cheese.*

Maximum Recommended Freezer Storage: *3 months*

SPEEDY CHILE CON CARNE

4 to 6 servings

Youngsters in particular are fond of chile con carne. This version is one they can enjoy preparing. Serve crackers or corn bread, dill pickles and relishes alongside the chile.

2 tablespoons oil
½ cup chopped onion
¼ cup chopped green pepper
1 pound ground beef
2 cups tomato sauce
2 cups cooked pinto beans
½ teaspoon garlic salt
1 teaspoon salt
1 teaspoon ground pure red chile
½ teaspoon ground comino
¼ teaspoon ground Mexican orégano

1 Heat oil in a large saucepan, then add the onion, green pepper and beef, and cook until meat is lightly browned.

2 Add tomato sauce and simmer for 5 minutes. Add pinto beans, garlic salt and salt. Stir in the ground chile, comino and orégano, and simmer for 30 minutes. Taste and adjust seasoning.

3 Ladle chile into soup bowls and serve.

Maximum Recommended Freezer Storage: *3 months*

RUFUS VALDEZ WORLD CHAMPIONSHIP CHILE

10 to 12 servings

A winner of the Texas Chile Cookoff one year.

4 large green chiles, or 4 ounces canned chiles
4 pounds flank steak, half ground, half cut into ½-inch cubes
2 pounds center-cut pork chops, trimmed from the bones and cut into ¼-inch cubes
1 teaspoon ground comino
1 teaspoon ground Mexican orégano
¼ cup rendered beef suet
4 cups chopped onions
½ cup chopped celery

★ ★

4 cups chopped tomatoes
4 cans (7 oz. each) chile salsa (a mixture of tomatoes, onion and chile)
2 garlic cloves, finely chopped
1 tablespoon ground mild red chile
2 tablespoons ground hot red chile

1 If green chiles are fresh, parch them following the instructions on page 21.
2 Put the beef in a skillet, adding a little fat if necessary, and cook, stirring often. Put the pork in another skillet and cook. Break up any lumps that form in either skillet. When the meats start to brown, cover and let cook for 45 minutes. Add half of the comino and orégano to each skillet and stir. Continue cooking for another 30 minutes.
3 Heat the suet in a 2-quart saucepan and add the onions and celery. Cook, stirring occasionally, for about 30 minutes. Add the tomatoes and chile salsa and continue cooking for another 30 minutes.
4 Sprinkle the tomato mixture with the garlic and ground chiles. Add the parched fresh or canned green chiles, chopped.
5 Combine the pork and beef. Add the tomato and spice mixture to the meats, stirring slowly. Cook slowly for about 1½ hours. Stir about every 10 minutes.

Variation: *For milder flavor, use 2 tablespoons ground mild red chile and 1 tablespoon ground hot red chile.*

Maximum Recommended Freezer Storage: *2 months*

★ ★

CHASEN'S CHILE   12 servings

Directly from Hollywood.

1¼ cups uncooked dried pinto beans
3 cups cold water
salt
10 medium-size tomatoes, peeled and chopped
1 tablespoon cooking oil
4 medium-size green peppers, chopped
4 medium-size sweet onions, chopped
2 tablespoons chopped garlic
½ cup finely chopped parsley
¼ pound (1 stick) butter
2½ pounds beef chuck, coarsely ground
1 pound pork, coarsely ground
½ cup ground pure red chile
1½ teaspoons ground black pepper
2 teaspoons crushed comino

1 Place the beans in a bowl, add 3 cups water, and let soak overnight.

2 Pour the beans and soaking water into a saucepan and bring to a boil. Cover and simmer until tender, about 1 hour. Stir occasionally to prevent scorching or burning. About 10 minutes before the beans are done, add salt to taste.

3 Drain the beans, reserving both the beans and the liquid. Pour the liquid into a saucepan and add the tomatoes. Set the beans aside. Bring the tomato mixture to a boil.

4 Heat the oil in a skillet and add the green peppers. Cook, stirring, for about 5 minutes. Add the onions and continue cooking, stirring, until the onions are translucent. Stir in the garlic and parsley.

5 Meanwhile, heat the butter in a casserole large enough to hold all the ingredients. Add the beef and pork and cook for about 15 minutes, stirring to break up any lumps. Sprinkle with the ground chile and cook, stirring occasionally, for about 10 minutes longer.

6 Add the green-pepper mixture and the tomato mixture to the meat. Add salt to taste, black pepper and comino. Cover and simmer for 1 hour. Stir often to prevent scorching or burning. A great deal of fat will rise to the top; this will be skimmed off later.

7 Uncover the casserole and simmer, stirring occasionally, for 30 minutes longer. Add the beans.

8 Tilt the casserole so that the fat runs downward. Skim off and discard as much of the fat as possible. Serve chile piping hot with garlic bread.

Note: *Chasen's recommends adding a dollop of whipped sour cream seasoned with lime juice and salt to taste.*

Freezing Hints: *Package in quantities of various serving sizes for greatest convenience.*

Maximum Recommended Freezer Storage: *2 months*

TAMALES

5 to 6 dozen tamales

The tantalizing flavor of homemade tamales far outshines the canned or frozen varieties. They are fun to make, especially if you have someone to help. Make the filling and masa the day before. In just one session, you can make a year's supply.

CHILE CON CARNE FILLING AND SAUCE

1½ pounds round steak or lean stewing beef, pork or chicken
2 tablespoons bacon drippings
1 tablespoon flour

1 cup Red Chile Sauce (p. 44) or ½ cup ground pure red chile
1 teaspoon salt
pinch of Mexican orégano
1 garlic clove, minced
1 to 2 cups meat stock

1 Simmer the meat in water to cover over medium to low heat. Cook until tender.

2 Cut meat into very tiny cubes, or chop in an electric blender at low speed. Heat the drippings in a large skillet. Add the meat and brown.

3 Add the flour, stirring constantly, and lightly brown the flour. Remove pan from the heat; when mixture is slightly cooled, add the chile sauce or ground chile; stir.

4 Season with salt, oregano and garlic. Add a scant cup of meat stock if using the chile sauce, more if using ground chile. Continue to add more, little by little, as the mixture simmers, stirring constantly. Cook for at least 30 minutes to blend the flavors. The sauce should be very thick and smooth.

Note: *Use more coarsely chopped meat in a thinner sauce to serve with the tamales. To save time, a double recipe of the filling can be prepared. After stuffing the tamales, thin the remaining half of the filling with beef stock for use as a sauce.*

TAMALE MASA
Cornmeal Mixture

6 cups masa
3½ cups warm water, approximately
2 cups lard
2 teaspoons salt
5 to 6 dozen rinsed and trimmed corn husks

1 Add warm water to the masa to make a very thick mixture that holds together, then allow it to stand. Beat the lard with an electric mixer at medium speed until the lard is fluffy and creamy. Add the salt. Combine the lard with the masa and mix well.

2 Meanwhile, soak the corn husks in warm water until soft. Spread each husk with about 2 tablespoons masa, making a rectangle about 4 by 3 inches and leaving at least a 2-inch margin of husk around the edges. Place a strip of chile con carne filling down the center of the masa. If desired, more masa may be added to the top of the chile con carne. Fold one side of the husk over the masa, covering the chile with the masa, then roll the husk to form a round tamale. Fold up the bottom of the husk and tie both ends with strips of corn husk, or just leave them folded.

3 If you plan to freeze the tamales, freeze them at this point, steaming them just before serving for best flavor. Otherwise, steam them immediately, or when desired for serving, by placing them on a rack in a pressure cooker,

deep-fryer or large kettle, standing them upright. Before the rack is completely filled, add water ½ inch deep in the bottom of the pan. Steam them under 15 pounds pressure for 20 minutes, or in a conventional steamer for 45 minutes.

4 When cooking frozen tamales, increase the cooking time by half. Serve with sauce, either thinned chile con carne in this recipe, or Red Chile Sauce plain or with pork added as mentioned under variations (p. 44).

Variation: *Half-size tamales can be made for hors d'oeuvre.*

Freezing Hints: *Package tamales in plastic bags, 12 per package or other suitable quantity. If packaging large quantities, keep track of the contents on a card. Package any leftover chile mixture or masa in rigid cartons, seal, and label.*

Maximum Recommended Freezer Storage: *1 year*

GREEN CORN TAMALES 24 tamales

These are a distinctive change from the more ordinary red chile tamales. When I met Paula Nietert of Douglas, Arizona, she had just spent the day preparing these. Paula and her husband were so enthusiastic about them I asked for the recipe immediately. When corn and chiles are in season, Paula buys bushels of them and freezes green corn tamales for year round enjoyment.

12 ears of fresh white or yellow corn
1 pound Monterey Jack cheese, grated
1 pound pure lard
½ pound butter
½ (scant) cup sugar
¼ cup light cream, or more
salt
2 dozen green chiles, parched (p. 21), and peeled
1 pound Cheddar or Longhorn cheese, grated

1 Chop stalk end off each ear of corn flush with the base of ear. Shuck, being careful to keep corn husks intact for later use. Wash husks and drain.

2 Cut corn off cobs. Grind corn with the Jack cheese in a meat grinder, blender or food processor.

3 Cream lard and butter to a smooth and fluffy consistency with an electric mixer at medium speed. Add the ground corn and cheese mixture, sugar, cream and salt to taste. Continue to mix with the electric mixer until mixture looks like whipped cream. Add more cream if mixture is dry.

4 Cut the roasted green chiles into long strips. Spread about 2 tablespoons of the corn mixture on each corn husk. Spread mixture out into a rectangle and allow at least 2 inches of husk to extend below the corn mixture and a few inches of margin on both sides of the husk. Place about 2 strips of green chile down the center of the corn mixture, then sprinkle with a few pinches of the grated Cheddar cheese.

5 Hold the two sides of the tamale together to make the corn mixture fold up around the filling. Then tuck one edge of the husk over the top of the tamale and roll, tying the ends with strips of corn husks. If preferred, the bottom end of the husk can be folded up over the bottom of the tamale before rolling. If you plan to freeze the tamales, freeze them at this point.

6 Place the tamales upright on a rack in a pressure cooker or large steaming kettle. Before the rack is completely filled with tamales, pour 1 to 2 cups water into the bottom of the pan, about ½ inch deep.

7 Steam at 15 pounds pressure for 25 minutes, or in conventional steamer for 45 minutes. Serve warm with Green Chile Sauce (p. 42), plain or with beef, pork or chicken added. These may be kept in the refrigerator for 3 to 4 days.

Freezing Hint: *See Freezing Hints, p. 106.*

Maximum Recommended Freezer Storage: *1 year*

FORT WORTH TAMALE PIE

4 to 6 servings

¼ cup chopped onion
1 tablespoon cooking oil
1 pound ground beef
8 ounces tomato sauce
½ teaspoon salt
1 teaspoon ground pure red chile, or more
12 tamales in husks
2 cups whole-kernel corn, drained
¼ cup chopped ripe olives
½ cup grated Monterey Jack cheese, or more

1 Brown the onion in the oil. Add beef and cook until lightly browned. Add tomato sauce and seasonings and mix well.

2 While the beef continues to cook, remove the tamales from the husks and mash well. Mix in the corn and olives.

3 Place half of the tamale mixture in a greased 2-quart casserole as the bottom layer of the pie.

4 Taste the beef mixture and adjust seasonings. Add meat to the casserole as the next layer. Place remaining tamale mixture on top. Sprinkle liberally with grated cheese. Bake at 350°F. for 1 hour.

Freezing Hints: *Crisscross 2 long pieces of foil or other durable wrap in the casserole; allow extra foil to hang over sides. Fill casserole and place in freezer. When the pie is frozen hard, remove from casserole and package airtight. To serve, replace in original casserole and thaw in the refrigerator for 4 to 6 hours. Bake as above. Or if still frozen, bake 3 hours.*

Maximum Recommended Freezer Storage: *2 months*

BUFFET TAMALE PIE
10 to 12 servings

An excellent dish for buffets; it can be frozen in several small casseroles.

8 cups water
3 cups yellow cornmeal
1 tablespoon salt
3 pounds ground beef
1 pound chorizo, chopped
1 small onion, finely chopped
½ cup chopped celery
½ cup chopped green pepper
1 cup whole-kernel corn
1 cup grated sharp cheese
1 cup pitted ripe olives
1 cup chicken broth
3½ cups canned tomatoes
1 tablespoon ground hot red chile
1 teaspoon ground comino
1 cup grated Monterey Jack cheese
12 stuffed green olives, sliced (optional)

1 Heat 5 cups of the water to boiling. Mix cornmeal, salt and remaining 3 cups water together and pour into boiling water, stirring constantly. Cook until thickened. Cover.

2 Before the mixture cools, use it to line a very large casserole dish. Reserve one-quarter of the mush for the topping.

3 Brown the ground beef, chorizo and onion. Add all remaining ingredients except the Monterey Jack cheese and the green olives.

4 Simmer mixture until somewhat thickened. Taste and adjust seasoning.

5 Spoon the mixture into the mush-lined casserole and top with reserved mush. Garnish top with grated Jack cheese, and with the sliced olives if desired. Bake at 325°F. for 2 or more hours.

Freezing Hint: *See Fort Worth Pie (above)*

Maximum Recommended Freezer Storage: *3 months*

TERRIFIC TAMALE PIE

6 servings

6 slices of bacon
1 pound ground beef
1 cup whole-kernel corn, fresh, frozen or canned
¼ cup chopped green chile
3 green onions, chopped
¼ cup cornmeal
¼ teaspoon orégano
1 teaspoon ground pure hot red chile
1 teaspoon salt
freshly ground black pepper
¼ teaspoon ground comino
8 ounces tomato sauce
Cornmeal Piecrust (recipe follows)
1 egg
¼ cup evaporated milk
½ teaspoon dry mustard
2 cups grated Monterey Jack cheese
4 stuffed olives, sliced

1 Fry bacon until crisp; break into large pieces. Set aside. Chill bacon drippings until firm for use in the crust.

2 Brown ground beef in a large skillet; drain off fat. Stir in next 10 ingredients. Reserve egg, evaporated milk, etc., for the top crust.

3 Prepare the piecrust, and use it to line a 9-inch pie pan. Place meat mixture in the pan. Bake at 425°F. for 25 minutes.

4 Meanwhile, combine egg, evaporated milk, mustard and cheese. Spread on top of the pie and decorate with the reserved bacon pieces and the sliced olives. Bake for 5 minutes longer, or until cheese melts. Let stand for 10 minutes, or until firm, before serving.

CORNMEAL PIECRUST

1 crust for 9-inch pie

1 cup all-purpose flour
2 tablespoons cornmeal
⅓ cup firm bacon drippings or other shortening
3 to 4 tablespoons cold water

1 Combine flour and cornmeal, then cut in bacon drippings. When mixture is granular, add the water, in small quantities to insure a flaky crust, until pastry is mixed.

2 Roll out on a floured surface to a circle 1½ times larger than an inverted 9-inch pie pan. Fit pastry into pan and form a fluted edge all around.

Maximum Recommended Freezer Storage: *2 months*

CHILES RELLENOS
Fried Stuffed Chiles

4 to 6 servings

There are many variations of chiles rellenos. I prefer Batter I (recipe follows) which yields a crisp, golden coating; especially good made with blue cornmeal. Serve chiles rellenos as a main dish with red or green chile sauce, posole or refritos, guacamole or tossed salad and sopaipillas.

12 large, mild green chiles with stems on, parched (p. 21) (if fresh ones are not available, buy three 4-ounce cans)
8 ounces Monterey Jack cheese, cut into long narrow strips
Batter (recipes follow)
vegetable oil or lard

1 Peel the chiles, leaving the stems on. Open a small slit below the stem and remove seeds if desired. Insert strips of cheese into the chiles, using care not to split them. Place on paper towels to drain. Prepare the batter of your choice. (You may prepare these in advance, then fry just before serving.)

2 Preheat 2 inches or more oil or lard to 375°F. in an electric skillet or deep-fryer; in a skillet on the range, test temperature of oil with a frying thermometer.

3 Dip the stuffed chiles into batter and fry until golden. Deep-frying assures rounder-looking chiles. Drain on absorbent paper towels.

Note: *Chiles rellenos are best when served piping hot with a side dish of red or green chile sauce. Any leftovers can be frozen and reheated under the broiler, or can be cut into 1-inch strips and served as hors d'oeuvre. Oil or lard can be strained and stored in the refrigerator for further use.*

Chiles rellenos can be fried ahead of time if absolutely necessary; however, they require only 10 minutes to fry if stuffed previously. They are much better freshly fried. If you must fry them ahead of time, drain them and place in a partly covered casserole in a warm oven until ready to serve.

Freezing Hint: *Place in layers separated by foil in rigid cartons.*

Maximum Recommended Freezer Storage: *3 months*

BATTER I

enough to coat 12 chiles

1 cup all-purpose flour
1 teaspoon baking powder
½ teaspoon salt
¾ cup blue, white or yellow cornmeal
1 cup milk
2 eggs, slightly beaten

1 Sift all-purpose flour with baking powder and salt, then add cornmeal.

2 Blend milk with slightly beaten eggs, then combine milk mixture with dry ingredients and blend together. (Sometimes more milk is needed to provide a smooth batter that clings to the chiles.)

BATTER II
(Egg and Flour Coating)

enough to coat 12 chiles

2 eggs
1½ cups all-purpose flour
½ teaspoon salt

1 Beat eggs well. Dip stuffed chiles into eggs, then dredge chiles with flour and salt mixed together.

BATTER III

enough to coat 12 chiles

4 eggs, separated
¾ teaspoon baking powder
4 tablespoons flour
¼ teaspoon salt

1 Beat the egg whites until stiff. Beat yolks until thick. Sift the dry ingredients together. Add to the yolks and blend well.

2 Fold beaten whites into the mixture.

BAKED CHILES RELLENOS

Some homemakers prefer to prepare this simplified version of chiles rellenos. They have good flavor, but I feel that the fried chiles are worth the effort. The baked ones lose their texture.

1 Prepare Chiles Rellenos using the recipe on page 110. Prepare 1 recipe of batter.

2 Grease an oblong baking dish 8 x 10 inches generously with butter. Place the cheese-stuffed chiles in a row in the dish.

3 Pour the batter over the chiles and bake in a 350°F. oven for about 30 minutes, until the batter is golden. Serve immediately. If desired, garnish the sides of the dish with coarsely chopped lettuce.

Freezing Information: *3 months*

SPICY MEAT-FILLED CHILES RELLENOS

4 to 6 servings

1 pound beef stew meat
4 cups water
1 teaspoon salt
2 teaspoons ground coriander
½ teaspoon ground cloves
2 garlic cloves, minced
2 tablespoons chopped onion
1 cup raisins
12 green chiles, or frozen or dried chiles
1 cup flour
1 teaspoon baking powder
½ teaspoon salt
2 eggs, slightly beaten
1 cup milk
3 egg whites (for dried chiles)
fat

1 Cook the meat in the water. When done, grind or purée meat in an electric blender. Mix in 1 teaspoon salt, the spices, garlic, onion and raisins.

2 Add enough of the meat broth to moisten. Cook until thick. Parch and peel fresh green chiles (p. 21), or soak dried chiles in a little warm water.

3 Stuff the fresh chiles with the meat mixture. If using dried chiles, stir them into the meat mixture and form the mixture into small oval shapes. Dip the ovals into flour.

4 Prepare the batter for the fresh chiles. Combine the flour, baking powder and ½ teaspoon salt, then add the eggs and milk, beating to form a smooth batter. Do not prepare batter for the dried chiles. Instead, prepare a meringue using 3 egg whites.

5 Heat 2 or more inches of fat to 375°F. Dip the fresh chiles into the batter, or the ovals with dried chiles into the meringue. Fry either to a golden brown. Drain and serve while still hot with or without a tomato sauce or chile salsa.

Freezing Information: *3 months*

POSOLE
Dried Corn with Pork and Red Chiles
12 servings

Posole, almost unheard of outside the Southwest, usually becomes an instant favorite. It seems better when frozen before serving as the flavors blend better and the texture becomes softer. You can serve it with a little sauce as a side dish or rather soupy as a stew. Served at New Year's, it brings legendary luck! There is one basic necessity when making it to assure tenderness: posole cannot be seasoned until it becomes soft. Remembering this, you will always have tender juicy posole. You may have to go to a store that carries Mexican specialty foods to get posole.

1 pound frozen posole, or 2 cups or 12 ounces dried posole
1 quart water, or more
2 pounds pork steak or roast, cut into small cubes
1 tablespoon salt
2 garlic cloves, minced
pinch of Mexican orégano
pinch of comino
6 red chile pods, dried, rinsed and deseeded

1 Cook the posole in the unseasoned water over a medium-low heat until it becomes soft; it usually requires 1½ to 2 hours. An electric deep-fryer set at simmer works very well for this. Brown the pork in a frying pan, then add 1 cup of water.

2 Combine posole with pork. Add remaining ingredients and cook the stew for 6 to 8 hours, or more. Ideally, this dish should be started the morning before it is to be served, to allow the flavors to develop.

Variations: *If desired, the chile pods can be left out and the posole can be served with a side dish of Red Chile Sauce (p. 44), so that each can make the posole as hot as desired. If chile pods are not available, substitute 2 or more tablespoons ground hot red chile. If serving posole with enchiladas, the sauce from them combines well with posole.*

Freezing Hints: *Place in rigid cartons. For greatest serving flexibility, use various sizes, to serve some single meals, etc.*

Maximum Recommended Freezer Storage: *8 months*

TEX-MEX POSOLE
Ground Beef and Hominy Casserole

4 to 6 servings

This variation of traditional posole retains a Southwestern flavor, but it is modified to use hominy. Serve as a main dish for buffets with crusty bread and a tossed green salad with avocado wedges and cherry tomatoes.

1 pound ground beef
1 medium-size onion, chopped
4 ounces chopped green chiles
2 tablespoons ground pure red chile (mild or hot, depending on your preference)
1 garlic clove, minced
¼ pound grated sharp cheese
3 or 4 corn tortillas, torn into pieces
3½ cups canned white hominy
salt
2 green onions, chopped

1 Brown the beef. Add the chopped onion and cook until onion is translucent. Add the green chiles, ground red chile, garlic, half of the grated cheese, the tortilla pieces and hominy. Mix well. Season with salt to taste and mix again.

2 Place the mixture in a greased 2-quart casserole (a Mexican earthenware one is nice). Bake at 350°F. for about 45 minutes. Add the rest of the cheese and chopped green onion. Heat until the cheese melts.

Maximum Recommended Freezer Storage: *4 months*

ENCHILADA CASSEROLE

4 servings

A modern version of enchiladas.

1 pound American cheese, cubed
13 ounces evaporated milk
1 pound ground beef
1 teaspoon salt
1 teaspoon garlic salt
12 corn tortillas
shortening
4 ounces chopped green chiles, fresh or frozen
½ cup chopped onion

1 Melt the cheese in the evaporated milk.

2 Fry ground beef until browned. Add salt and garlic salt. Pour off fat.

3 Dip tortillas into ½ inch of hot shortening on each side until soft.

4 Place ingredients in a greased 2-quart casserole dish, starting with tortillas. Add ground beef, chiles and onion; repeat.

5 Pour cheese mixture over entire dish and cover.

6 Bake in a 350°F. oven for 25 to 30 minutes.

Variations: *Add 2 cups cooked pinto beans for added flavor. Add more green chiles if desired.*

Freezing Hint: *See Buffet Tamale Pie (p. 108)*

Maximum Recommended Freezer Storage: *4 to 6 months*

CACEROLA

4 servings

This dish is South American in origin. Serve with Marinated Vegetable Salad with Blue-Cheese Dressing (p. 70).

1½ pounds lean ground beef
1 medium-size onion, chopped
1 teaspoon instant coffee powder or more
1 teaspoon ground pure red chile
1 teaspoon salt
¼ teaspoon black pepper
2 cups tomato sauce
8 corn tortillas
3 ounces cream cheese
½ cup grated Monterey Jack or Cheddar cheese
shredded lettuce and black or stuffed olives for garnish (optional)

1 Brown the beef and onion in a skillet. Drain off fat. Stir in coffee powder and seasonings and 1 cup of tomato sauce. Simmer for 5 minutes.

2 Butter a shallow pottery baking dish. Spread tortillas with cream cheese, then top with some of the meat mixture.

3 Fold each tortilla in half and place in the baking dish with folded side of tortilla on the bottom, or open side up. Fill in spaces around tortillas with remaining meat mixture.

4 Pour remaining cup of tomato sauce evenly over the casserole. Sprinkle with cheese. Bake at 350°F. for 20 minutes or until hot. Garnish the edge of casserole with finely shredded lettuce and black or stuffed olives, if desired.

Freezing Hints: *See Buffet Tamale Pie (p. 108)*

Maximum Recommended Freezer Storage: *2 months*

FRITO PIE
4 servings

Straight from Big D, this casserole is a great way to use up "too-small" bits of any kind of corn chips or tostados. Serve with a crisp green salad.

2½ cups crushed tostados
1 large onion, finely chopped
2 cups chile or red chile (any kind, even leftover chile stew)
1 cup grated sharp Cheddar cheese

1 Grease a 1½- or 2-quart casserole generously. Place a layer of corn chips in casserole, using 1½ cups of the chips. Preheat oven to 350°F.

2 Add the onion in an even layer. Spread the chile evenly over the onion. Sprinkle with remaining corn chips and top with grated cheese. Bake in the preheated oven for 15 minutes, or until cheese is melted and chile is bubbly.

Not Recommended for Freezing

MEXI-CHILE CASSEROLE
4 to 6 servings

Traveling with "food fixings" is almost a way of life in the Southwest, with the great distances separating friends and recreational areas. Spicy Mexican-inspired casseroles are popular to prepare on sight to satisfy hearty appetites.

4 cups corn chips
2 cups shredded Monterey Jack or Cheddar cheese
15 ounces canned chile with beans
15 ounces canned enchilada sauce
8 ounces canned tomato sauce
1 medium-size onion, chopped
½ cup chopped green chiles, or 4 ounces canned chiles
1 cup sour cream

1 Combine 3 cups corn chips and 1½ cups cheese with the rest of the ingredients. Spread mixture evenly in a greased 2- to 3-quart baking dish.

2 Bake uncovered at 350°F. for 15 to 20 minutes, or until hot. Spread top with sour cream and sprinkle with remaining cheese.

3 Decorate edges of casserole with remaining cup of corn chips. Bake 5 minutes longer.

Not Recommended for Freezing

CHILE-CHICKEN CASSEROLE

4 to 6 servings

Prepare several of these casseroles for the freezer for easy company dinners or fun family nights when you, the cook, can enjoy your own meal in leisure.

1 frying chicken, 2½ to 3 pounds
2 cups finely chopped celery
1 small carrot, finely chopped
1 medium-size onion, chopped
1 garlic clove, minced
pinch of cilantro
2 teaspoons salt
freshly ground black pepper
½ teaspoon ground thyme
3 tablespoons flour
¼ cup cold water
4 cups tostados or corn chips (crumbly ones work fine)
1 cup fresh whole green chiles, parched and peeled (p. 21), or frozen or canned chiles
1 cup grated Cheddar or Monterey Jack cheese

1 Put the chicken in a cooking pot and add the celery, carrot, onion, garlic, cilantro, salt, a pinch of pepper and the thyme. Add just enough water to cover. Simmer until very tender, about 1 hour. Leg joints should move easily. Strain the cooking broth and reserve 3 cups.

2 Remove bones and skin from chicken, and cut meat into medium-size chunks.

3 Strain the broth and measure 3 cups into a saucepan. Mix the flour with the cold water until smooth. Stir into the broth and cook until slightly thickened, about 10 minutes.

4 Butter a large, shallow pottery casserole. Fill it with layers of tostados, chiles and chicken, and drizzle broth over the layers. Top with cheese. Bake at 375°F. for about 30 minutes, or freeze for baking later.

Variation: *Whole tortillas can be substituted for the tostados. Use about 12 for 1 recipe.*

Freezing Hint: *See Buffet Tamale Pie (p. 108)*

Maximum Recommended Freezer Storage: *6 months*

BEEF MAIN DISHES

Beef is definitely the most popular meat in the Southwest. Dating from the days of the cattle drives, beef has been consumed in generous quantities just for its own sake.

Even today local steak houses feature 64-ounce T-bones as a standard item. Picadillo is perhaps the most unique dish in this chapter, with the roasts, ground beef and kabobs each having a Tex-Mex touch.

PECOS RIVER POT ROAST

4 servings

Southwesterners have their own version of pot roast; it is served with rice, a green vegetable and hard crusty Mexican rolls.

2½ pounds Swiss steak or arm roast, cut 2 inches thick
½ cup flour
3 tablespoons bacon drippings
¾ teaspoon salt
1 large onion, sliced and separated into rings
1 garlic clove, minced
2 cups canned whole tomatoes
2 green chiles, finely chopped
pinch of Mexican orégano

1 Flour the beef and brown in hot drippings. Season with the salt.

2 Place in a baking dish and add the remaining ingredients.

3 Pot-roast, basting occasionally and adding water if necessary. The meat should be fork tender when ready to serve. The gravy is excellent served with the meat and steamed rice.

Maximum Recommended Freezer Storage: *8 months*

PICADILLO
Spicy Beef

4 servings

This Southwestern favorite from Texas has an unusual sweet, spicy flavor. Serve it with rice, a green vegetable and fruit salad.

1 pound lean beef or steak, coarsely chopped, or good-quality lean pork roast
1 medium-size onion, finely chopped
2 large fresh tomatoes, peeled and chopped, or 1 cup solid-pack canned tomatoes
1 garlic clove, crushed
2 tablespoons vinegar
1 teaspoon sugar
1 teaspoon ground cinnamon
pinch of ground cloves
¼ teaspoon ground comino
1 teaspoon salt
½ cup seedless raisins, plumped in ¼ cup hot stock
½ cup slivered blanched almonds

1 Brown the meat over medium heat. After meat begins to cook and some of the fat begins to cook out, add the onion. Cook until onion is translucent. Drain off excess fat, if any.

2 Add all remaining ingredients except almonds. Simmer for about 30 minutes. Add the almonds just before serving; use them as a garnish for the top of the dish.

Maximum Recommended Freezer Storage: *2 months*

MEXICAN BEEF KABOBS   4 to 6 servings

Serve as a main dish or snack. Favorite accompaniments are New Mexican Corn Custard (p. 158), Broiled Tomato Halves (p. 156), a green salad and crusty garlic bread.

½ cup chopped onion
1 tablespoon olive oil
1 cup red-wine vinegar
½ teaspoon salt
½ teaspoon each of Mexican orégano, comino, ground pure red chile, ground cloves, ground cinnamon, pepper
1 garlic clove, minced
1½ pounds lean sirloin steak, cut into 1½-inch cubes
8 to 10 small onions, parboiled
8 to 12 cherry pepper pickles

1 Cook onion in olive oil until translucent but not brown. Add vinegar, seasoning and garlic. Cover pan and allow to simmer for 20 minutes; cool.

2 Add meat and marinate at room temperature for at least 1 hour.

3 Skewer meat cubes alternately with the onions and peppers. Brush with the marinade. Broil in the oven or on an outdoor grill, basting often until done to your liking.

Maximum Recommended Freezer Storage: *2 months*

SOUTHWESTERN SWISS STEAK

4 to 6 servings

For a different Swiss steak, try this recipe. Serve wheat-flour tortillas for "sopping up" the flavorful sauce.

1 cup dry white wine
3 tablespoons red wine or wine vinegar
2 or more canned green chiles, finely chopped (not jalapenos)
1 tablespoon brown sugar
1 teaspoon salt
1 garlic clove, minced
2 pounds beef round steak, cut 1½ to 2 inches thick
1 tablespoon shortening
½ cup beef bouillon
¼ cup bottled condiment chile sauce
¼ cup thinly sliced onion rings, or more
½ cup pitted ripe olives
2 fresh tomatoes, quartered
avocado wedges, drizzled with lime juice
parsley sprigs

1 Mix together first 6 ingredients and pour into a shallow pan large enough for the beef. Trim excess fat from meat and pierce it deeply on both sides several times, using a meat fork.

2 Marinate the meat in the mixture in refrigerator overnight. Next day, drain meat and measure out 1 cup of the marinade.

3 Heat shortening in a large frypan. Brown meat on both sides. Add reserved marinade, the bouillon, chile sauce and onion rings.

4 Cover pan and simmer meat for 1¼ to 1½ hours, until tender. (Meat can be baked in a 325°F. oven for the same length of time.)

5 Skim off fat. Simmer uncovered, if necessary, to reduce the cooking juices and allow them to thicken. Then stir in two-thirds of the black olives.

6 Place meat on a heated platter. Top with some of the sauce, and pour the rest into a separate serving dish. Garnish around the edge of the steak with fresh tomato wedges, remaining olives, avocado wedges and parsley.

Freezing Hints: *Steak can be frozen in the marinade, ready for popping into the oven. Oven can be set to turn on automatically. If you should have any leftovers, they can be frozen.*

Maximum Recommended Freezer Storage: *8 months*

AVOCADO-STUFFED HAMBURGERS

4 servings

These surprise hamburgers are great for buffets, luncheons and patio suppers.

1¼ pounds very lean ground beef
⅓ cup fine dry bread crumbs
1¼ cups tomato juice
1 egg, beaten
1 small onion, finely grated
3 teaspoons ground pure red chile, or more
½ teaspoon ground Mexican orégano
1 teaspoon salt
1½ tablespoons Worcestershire sauce
1 small avocado, peeled, pitted and thinly sliced
¾ cup grated Monterey Jack cheese
4 ounces canned chopped green chiles
¼ teaspoon seasoning salt

1 Place the meat in a mixing bowl and stir with a fork to crumble. Add bread crumbs, ¼ cup tomato juice, egg, onion, 2 teaspoons ground chile, seasonings and Worcestershire sauce. Stir and mix until very well blended.

2 Divide the meat mixture into 8 equal parts and roll or pat out each to form a round patty ⅜ inch thick.

3 If baking immediately, preheat the oven to 400°F. Lightly grease a 9-inch-square pan. Place 4 patties on the pan, then in the center of each, place one fourth of the avocado slices and grated cheese. Add 1 tablespoon of green chile to each and reserve the rest. Top each patty with a second patty and press the edges together to seal.

4 At this point the stuffed hamburgers can be chilled for baking and serving up to 8 hours later. If serving immediately, place the burgers in the preheated oven and bake until they are only slightly pink on the inside of the burger, 15 to 20 minutes.

5 Meanwhile, prepare the sauce for topping the burgers. Place remaining tomato juice, the seasoning salt, remaining ground red chile and the rest of the green chiles in a saucepan over medium heat and simmer while the burgers bake. Serve each patty with some sauce spooned over the top.

Not Recommended for Freezing

NEW MEXICAN HAMBURGERS

4 servings

1 pound ground beef
generous dash of black pepper
1 teaspoon ground pure red chile
1 egg, beaten
½ medium-size onion, finely chopped
1 small garlic clove, crushed
½ teaspoon salt
dash of Tabasco
2 tablespoons chopped green chile
4 slices of Monterey Jack cheese
4 sesame hamburger buns
butter
basil or tarragon

1 Mix the beef with the next 8 ingredients. Shape into 4 flat patties. Broil in an oven or over charcoal to desired doneness.

2 Just before serving the burgers, melt a slice of cheese on top. Butter the buns and sprinkle with crushed tarragon or basil. Toast until lightly browned. Serve immediately. For a real New Mexican twist, serve fresh Salsa (p. 42) on the side.

Maximum Recommended Freezer Storage: *2 months*

MEXICAN MEAT LOAF

4 servings

Serve this dish with New Mexican Corn Custard or Elote (p. 158) and a crisp green salad.

1 pound ground beef
½ pound ground fresh pork
1 onion, finely chopped
1 garlic clove, minced
1 egg, slightly beaten
½ cup oatmeal, bread or cracker crumbs
1 teaspoon salt
pinch of comino
pinch of dried mint (optional)
8 ounces tomato sauce
¼ pound Monterey Jack cheese, grated
Spanish stuffed olives (optional)

1 Preheat oven to 325°F. Mix together all ingredients except 4 ounces of the tomato sauce, the cheese and olives. Mold into a loaf shape and place in a buttered baking dish.

2 Top with remaining tomato sauce and the cheese.

3 Bake for 1 hour. Garnish with halved stuffed Spanish olives.

Maximum Recommended Freezer Storage: *2 months*

PORK MAIN DISHES

Pork is most popular with the Spanish Americans and Mexicans. They cook very creatively with it, combining it with red chile for such specialties as carne adobada, chorizo and Mexican spareribs.

CARNE ADOBADA
Chile-Marinated Pork

10 to 12 servings

For a traditional menu, serve sopaipillas or corn bread, a crisp green salad laced with a tart dressing, and cheese-topped refritos. Natillas or flan will nicely complete the meal.

1 cup chile caribe (p. 20)
4 cups water
2 teaspoons salt
3 garlic cloves, chopped
2 tablespoons ground Mexican orégano
2 tablespoons ground comino
5 pounds fresh pork, thinly sliced (loin chops are excellent)

1 Combine chile caribe and water in a blender container and whirl until mixed into a sauce. Add salt, garlic, orégano and comino to the sauce; mix well.

2 Trim excess fat from the pork and lay slices in a flat baking dish. Cover with the sauce; turn the meat once to coat evenly on both sides. If possible, allow to marinate in the refrigerator overnight.

3 To cook, cover the baking dish with a lid or sheet of aluminum foil and bake at 325°F. for 30 minutes. Uncover and bake for 30 minutes more, basting periodically.

Note: *Any remaining pork will keep in the refrigerator for up to 1 week. If desired, the pork will freeze well in the marinade. Any unused marinade also will freeze well.*

Variation: *This chile makes very good filling for spicy tacos or burritos.*

Maximum Recommended Freezer Storage: *3 months*

MEXICAN SPARERIBS

4 servings

3 pounds lean pork spareribs
4 garlic cloves, minced
2 teaspoons salt
6 tablespoons olive oil, or half olive oil, half salad oil
dash of freshly ground pepper
4 tablespoons vinegar
2 teaspoons ground Mexican oregano
2 cups Red Chile Sauce (p. 44)
2 tablespoons minced onion

1 Slice ribs into individual portions and place in a large baking dish. Sprinkle ribs with garlic, salt, oil, pepper, vinegar and orégano. Allow to marinate at room temperature for about 3 hours.

2 Pour red chile sauce over the ribs. Sprinkle with onion.

3 Place in a 350°F. oven and bake for about 2 hours, or until done.

Maximum Recommended Freezer Storage: *3 months*

NEW MEXICAN PORK CHOP BAKE
4 to 6 servings

2 tablespoons butter or bacon drippings
1 large onion, sliced into rings
4 to 6 large lean pork chops
3 parched green chiles, peeled and chopped (p. 21), or 4 ounces canned green chiles
1 cup uncooked rice
3 cups water
4 cups stewed tomatoes
1 teaspoon ground Mexican orégano
½ teaspoon ground comino
1 garlic clove, crushed
1 teaspoon salt

1 Melt butter or drippings in a large deep skillet or casserole. Sauté onion rings until they become translucent. Push aside in the pan.

2 Quickly brown the pork chops in the same pan and remove to a plate. Add the green chiles to the onion and mix, then top each pork chop with some of the mixture.

3 Add the rice to the pan; cover with the water and stewed tomatoes. Stir in the seasonings and top with the pork chops. Cover. Baste twice while they bake.

4 Bake in a 350°F. oven for 1 hour.

Maximum Recommended Freezer Storage: *3 months*

CHORIZO

Mexican Sausage   20 sausages or 2⅔ pounds bulk sausage

For outstanding egg or tortilla combinations, you may wish to make your own chorizo if you cannot purchase it where you live. A food processor or meat grinder makes the task easy. For authentic links, purchase pork casings, usually available at ethnic meat markets or by ordering from your butcher. I've generally made bulk sausage, as it is much easier. Sausage has to be taken out of the casing for most uses anyway.

20 sausage casings
vinegar
2 pounds lean pork trimmings
8 ounces beef or pork fat
2 medium-size onions, quartered
8 garlic cloves, pushed through a garlic press
½ cup cider vinegar
¼ cup tequila (optional)
¼ cup ground red chile, mild or hot
1 teaspoon ground cinnamon
1½ teaspoons ground comino
1 teaspoon ground Mexican orégano
1 tablespoon salt

1 Clean the casings, rinse well with water, then pour vinegar through them. Set aside.

2 Use a food processor or the coarse blade of a meat grinder, grind the meat and fat. Add the onions, garlic, vinegar, tequila and seasonings, using the hotness of chile powder your family and guests will prefer.

3 Stuff the casings. First cut the casing into 3-foot lengths and tie one end together. Use either a funnel or filling tube to fill the lengths. Tie at about 4-inch intervals with heavy thread.

4 Place on a cookie sheet covered with wax paper. Set on the counter for about 2 hours, then refrigerate.

5 After a day, freeze what you will not use within a week or two. Mixture should ripen for at least 8 hours before using.

Notes: *If you have no food processor or grinder, buy triple-ground pork.*
Prepare the recipe once and taste for the mildness or hotness of the ground red chile. Adjust to suit your taste for the next time you make sausage.

Freezing Hints: *Mold the sausage into ½-pound lumps and freeze between pieces of foil inside a heavy plastic bag.*

Maximum Recommended Freezer Storage: *3 months*

CHILE COLORADO CON CARNE DE PUERCO
Red Chile with Pork

4 to 5 servings

Natives of the Rio Grande area have long savored the goodness of this main dish in the fall and winter. They usually eat this poured over stewed pinto beans and serve hot puffy sopaipillas dripping with honey to complete the meal.

2 tablespoons lard
1 pound lean pork, cut into small cubes
2 tablespoons flour
1 teaspoon salt
1½ cups Red Chile Sauce (p. 44)
1 garlic clove, crushed
dash of ground Mexican orégano
dash of ground comino

1 Melt the lard in a heavy skillet, then add the pork cubes and fry until lightly browned.

2 Stir in the flour and salt. Add remaining ingredients, cover, and simmer for 30 to 45 minutes.

Variations: *Cubed or ground beef may be used. Leftover roast, cubed, may be used. Venison or similar game also works well, but pork is traditional.*

Maximum Recommended Freezer Storage: *3 months*

MEXICAN LUNCHEON

8 servings

Children love this!

1 pound bulk sausage
1 cup diced onion
1 cup diced green chiles or sweet peppers
2 cups uncooked elbow macaroni
2 cups canned tomatoes
1 cup sour cream
1 cup milk
2 tablespoons sugar
2 tablespoons ground pure red chile
1 teaspoon salt

1 Brown the sausage, onion and green chile or sweet peppers.

2 Add the macaroni, tomatoes, sour cream, milk, sugar and seasonings. Cover and simmer for 20 to 25 minutes, or until macaroni is tender.

Not Recommended for Freezing

POULTRY MAIN DISHES

The Spanish influence is pervasive in almost all poultry dishes from the border states. I've always been exceptionally fond of both pollo con crema and pollo mole. The subtly flavored crema sauce contrasts strikingly with the mole—yet each is wonderfully tasty. The other poultry specialties are favorites, each possessing the flavor accents that spell Southwestern.

ARROZ CON POLLO
Chicken with Rice and Vegetable Sauce   8 to 10 servings

A Spanish chicken dish that is a favorite in Mexico and the border states.

¼ cup olive oil, or more
2 young frying chickens, about 2½ pounds each, cut into individual pieces
2 teaspoons salt
6 chorizo sausage links
4 cups uncooked long-grain rice
2 teaspoons minced garlic
1 large onion, finely chopped
1 large green bell pepper, finely chopped
¼ teaspoon Mexican saffron, crumbled
6 cups chicken stock, or more
6 large red ripe tomatoes, peeled and chopped
10 ounces slightly cooked frozen sweet peas
4 ounces pimiento strips

1 Pour the oil into a large heavy frying pan and heat to medium-high temperature. Add the chicken pieces and sprinkle with salt. You may need to fry part at a time. Add more oil if needed. Brown each piece and transfer to a large earthenware baking dish.

2 In the same oil, brown the chorizo links and remove to the baking dish, spacing the sausages among the chicken pieces. Add half of the rice, making an even layer.

3 In the same fat, sauté the garlic, onion and bell pepper, stirring to cook evenly. When the vegetables are limp, distribute them evenly over the top of the chicken, sausage and rice, then spoon remaining rice over the top.

4 Add the saffron to the chicken stock and mix well. Pour over the rice. Add the chopped tomatoes. Cover tightly and bake at 350°F. for 1½ hours without peeking.

5 Check to be sure rice is fluffy and the chicken pieces well done. If not, bake a little longer. About 30 minutes before serving, transfer to a serving dish if the baking dish is not suitable for serving. Garnish top with the peas and pimiento strips.

POLLO MOLE
Chicken in Spicy Tomato and Chocolate Sauce 6 servings

Mexico's most unusual dish, mole, is often prepared with chicken, although turkey can be used. Chicken or turkey meat can be used as a filling for tamales, which are then served with the mole sauce.

1 roasting chicken, 4 pounds, cut up
celery tops
1 carrot, quartered
½ onion, quartered
2½ teaspoons salt
1 slice of dry bread
2 tablespoons seedless raisins
½ ounce (½ square) unsweetened chocolate
3 tablespoons blanched almonds
2 tablespoons minced onions
1 medium-size green pepper, finely chopped
1 large fresh tomato, quartered
1 garlic clove, minced
3 tablespoons flour
1 tablespoon ground hot red chile
¼ teaspoon ground cinnamon
¼ teaspoon ground cloves
2½ cups chicken stock

1 Cover chicken with cold water. Add celery tops, carrot, onion and 2 teaspoons salt. Cook until tender. Set aside and cool.

2 Grind bread, raisins, chocolate, almonds, onion, green pepper, tomato and garlic, using a food processor or electric blender.

3 Stir in flour and spices, then add 2½ cups chicken stock and mix until well blended.

4 Cook sauce until slightly thickened. Add chicken pieces and simmer gently for 30 minutes, basting frequently.

Maximum Recommended Freezer Storage: *6 months*

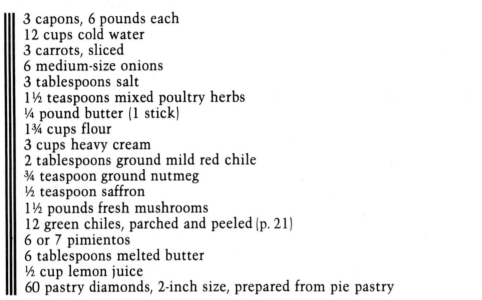

WEDDING CHICKEN

20 servings

There needn't be a wedding in the family to enjoy this; it is perfect for a buffet luncheon or dinner.

3 capons, 6 pounds each
12 cups cold water
3 carrots, sliced
6 medium-size onions
3 tablespoons salt
1½ teaspoons mixed poultry herbs
¼ pound butter (1 stick)
1¾ cups flour
3 cups heavy cream
2 tablespoons ground mild red chile
¾ teaspoon ground nutmeg
½ teaspoon saffron
1½ pounds fresh mushrooms
12 green chiles, parched and peeled (p. 21)
6 or 7 pimientos
6 tablespoons melted butter
½ cup lemon juice
60 pastry diamonds, 2-inch size, prepared from pie pastry

1 Place each whole capon in a large kettle. Add 4 cups cold water to each kettle along with 1 carrot, 1 onion, halved, 1 teaspoon salt and ½ teaspoon mixed poultry herbs. Simmer for about 1 hour, or until capons are tender. Cool in the broth.

2 Strip meat from the skin and bones and cut into bite-size pieces. Return the bones to the broth and simmer for at least 1 hour longer. Strain and chill the broth. (The giblets and the skin are not used for this dish.) When broth is cold, skim fat from the surface. Reserve 3 cups broth for the sauce.

3 In a large heavy pan combine ¼ pound butter and the flour to make a thick *roux*. When butter is melted and combined with flour, add the reserved 3 cups chicken broth and the heavy cream. Stir to make a thick, creamy sauce. Season it with 2 tablespoons salt, the red chile, nutmeg and saffron. Blend well. Whirl in an electric blender until completely smooth. Cool.

4 Wipe off mushrooms with a damp cloth, trim base of stems, then slice thinly. Peel and finely chop remaining onions; chop the green chiles and the pimientos. Sauté all vegetables in 6 tablespoons melted butter until onions are translucent. Drain vegetables on paper toweling.

5 Combine chicken and vegetables with the sauce. The recipe can be prepared up to this point the day before serving or can be frozen for later use.

6 To serve, heat over simmering water or very low heat for about 1 hour. Just

before serving, add the lemon juice and mix well. Serve over pastry diamonds, allowing 3 pieces to a serving.

Maximum Recommended Freezer Storage: *6 months*

SPANISH CHICKEN

4 servings

1 stewing chicken, 3 to 4 pounds, cut as for frying
¼ pound butter
3 medium-size onions, chopped
1 large green bell pepper, chopped
4 ounces canned chopped pimientos
1 tablespoon ground mild red chile, or more
½ teaspoon caraway seeds
2 teaspoons salt
½ teaspoon freshly ground black pepper
3 tomatoes, cut into thin wedges
1 cup chicken broth, or more as needed
1 cup sour cream
3 tablespoons flour
2 tablespoons snipped fresh parsley
½ cup pitted black olives, cut into rings

1 Place cut-up chicken in a large casserole that has been generously buttered.

2 Melt butter in a frying pan and lightly sauté the onions and green pepper. When limp, add pimientos and cook until golden. Pour evenly over the chicken.

3 Season with the chile, caraway seeds, salt and pepper. Cover with the tomatoes and chicken broth. Add more chicken broth if needed during baking. Bake in a 350°F. oven for 1½ hours, or until tender.

4 When the chicken is tender when pierced with a fork, remove casserole from oven and remove chicken from the sauce.

5 Combine the sour cream with the flour and stir into the sauce in the casserole dish. Stir until well blended. Place over medium heat and simmer until thickened.

6 Serve the chicken drizzled with the sauce and sprinkled with freshly snipped parsley and black olive rings. A side dish of rice is a must for the gravy.

Maximum Recommended Freezer Storage: *4 months*

POLLO CON CREMA
Chicken in Cream Sauce

4 servings

Serve pollo con crema over plain or wild rice accompanied by a generous tossed salad, herb-buttered squash and crusty rolls.

1 frying chicken, 2½ pounds, cut up
salt
1 garlic clove, minced
1 medium-size onion, coarsely chopped
1 large onion, finely chopped
¼ pound butter
1 tablespoon flour
2 cups light cream
pepper
4 ounces canned pimientos, chopped

1 Cook frying chicken in 2 cups water, lightly salted. Add the garlic and medium-size onion. Cook until the chicken is tender. Reserve the broth for cooking rice.

2 Sauté the chopped large onion in butter. When onion is translucent, stir in the flour. Then add the cream, salt and pepper to taste and pimientos. Combine well. Sauce can be refrigerated at this point for serving later.

3 Debone the chicken (or leave on bones if preferred) and place the meat in the sauce. Simmer for 10 minutes. Serve over plain or wild rice.

Maximum Recommended Freezer Storage: *6 months*

GALLINA RELLENA
Stuffed Chicken

4 servings

At one time this recipe was prepared only on feast days and holidays. I prefer to baste with the chocolate baste, but if you wish a milder flavor, try basting with butter. Serve with a tossed green salad, warm Mexican hard rolls and a full-bodied red wine. Finish with rich chocolate ice cream sprinkled with almonds.

1 young chicken, 3 pounds
1 teaspoon salt
½ pound ground beef
1 cup raisins
½ cup piñóns or slivered blanched almonds
1 ounce (1 square) unsweetened chocolate
1 teaspoon coriander seeds
½ teaspoon ground cinnamon
¼ teaspoon ground cloves
½ cup meat stock
salt
¼ cup red wine
melted butter, if not using baste
Chocolate Baste (recipe follows)

1 Rinse and dress the chicken. Lightly sprinkle cavity with 1 teaspoon salt.

2 Sauté the ground beef. Drain off excess fat and reserve fat for the baste, if using baste. Combine the cooked beef with the raisins, nuts, chocolate, spices, meat stock and salt to taste. Cook until mixture thickens slightly.

3 Add wine and bring to a boil, then simmer briefly. Use the mixture to stuff the chicken. Truss the bird. Baste with melted butter or prepare baste. Brush periodically with whichever you use as the chicken bakes. Bake the chicken in a 350°F. oven for 1½ hours.

CHOCOLATE BASTE

½ cup beef bouillon
¼ cup red wine
¼ teaspoon ground cinnamon
1 ounce (1 square) unsweetened chocolate
pinch of ground cloves
¼ cup beef fat (from frying ground beef)

1 Mix all ingredients together and beat until chocolate is melted and everything is well combined. Brush onto bird before baking and periodically during the baking process. Serve any remaining baste in a gravy boat with the chicken.

Maximum Recommended Freezer Storage: *6 months*

M-M CHICKEN

4 to 6 servings

This recipe is one of my daughter Amy's favorite dinner requests. Serve with confetti rice made by tossing cooked rice with butter, salt, chopped red and green pepper; and a sliced orange, onion-ring and lettuce salad, laced with poppy-seed dressing.

1 frying chicken, 3 pounds, cut into serving pieces
¼ cup ground mild red chile
1 teaspoon ground Mexican orégano
1 teaspoon ground comino
1 teaspoon salt
2 garlic cloves, crushed

1 Lightly oil a large flat baking dish.

2 Place chicken pieces in a single layer in the pan. Combine the other ingredients and sprinkle half over the chicken. Bake uncovered at 375°F. for 30 minutes.

3 Turn each chicken piece over and sprinkle with remaining seasoning mix. Bake for an additional 30 minutes. Spoon drippings over the chicken before serving.

Maximum Recommended Freezer Storage: *3 months*

FISH & SHELLFISH MAIN DISHES

Fish and shellfish are served sparingly in the Southwest. In Mexico with its two coasts, several delicious fish and shellfish dishes were developed that have made their way into the border states. The most popular of these dishes are included here.

SOUTHWESTERN CEVICHE

4 servings as entrée, 8 as appetizer

With increasing availability of fresh seafood in the border states, dishes such as this one have gained popularity. This can be served as an appetizer or as an entrée for a light meal.

1¼ pounds fresh bay scallops
¾ cup freshly squeezed lime juice, 5 or 6 limes
3 to 4 green chiles, parched (p. 21), peeled and chopped
4 scallions, finely chopped, or ½ cup chopped red Spanish onion
3 medium-size fresh tomatoes, peeled, seeded, and cut into very fine wedges
½ teaspoon sea salt
generous pinch of ground Mexican orégano
3 tablespoons olive oil
1 tablespoon chopped fresh cilantro
4 lettuce cups
1 avocado, peeled, pitted and sliced into wedges

1 Place the scallops in a shallow wide-bottomed glass container such as a pie plate or casserole.

2 Pour the lime juice evenly over the scallops. Cover and place in the refrigerator for about 2 hours. Stir once or twice.

3 Combine the remaining ingredients except lettuce and avocado and stir into the scallops. Allow to marinate for at least 1 hour longer, no more than 2 hours. Stir occasionally.

4 Serve in lettuce cups in chilled sherbet dishes or wineglasses or on clear glass plates. Garnish with avocado wedges.

Variation: *Fresh sweet red pepper strips may be substituted for the avocado as a garnish. A topping of additional minced fresh cilantro is good.*

ROCKY MOUNTAIN GRILLED TROUT

4 servings

Fresh from the icy streams, trout prepared in this manner are excellent. Small salmon are also great.

4 whole fresh trout, each 10 to 12 inches long
1 teaspoon minced fresh basil, or ½ teaspoon crushed dried basil
1 teaspoon minced fresh tarragon, or ½ teaspoon crushed dried tarragon
¼ teaspoon ground comino

1 teaspoon salt
freshly ground black pepper or ground mild red chile
1 large or 2 small fresh limes, cut into rounds complete with rind
¼ cup finely chopped purple Spanish onion
¼ pound sweet butter, melted
1 lime, cut into 4 wedges
4 parsley sprigs

1 Heat an outdoor grill or preheat a broiler.

2 Prepare the trout; rinse out the inside cavity and remove any excess membranes. Dry. Combine herbs and seasonings. Mix half with lime rounds and onion and place some in each cavity in layers. Drizzle half of the melted butter evenly over the mixture in the cavities. Skewer the openings closed.

3 Brush one side of each fish with butter. Sprinkle with some of remaining herbs and seasonings. Place on the grill and brown one side. Brush the second side of each trout with butter and seasonings. Grill until browned. Trout is done when outside is golden and flesh is soft to the touch. An inserted skewer should reveal juicy, flaky flesh. Serve while hot with wedges of lime and parsley sprigs.

Variation: *If broiling salmon, remove the skin before serving. Serve with a pitcher of melted sweet butter flavored with a few drops of liquid smoke.*

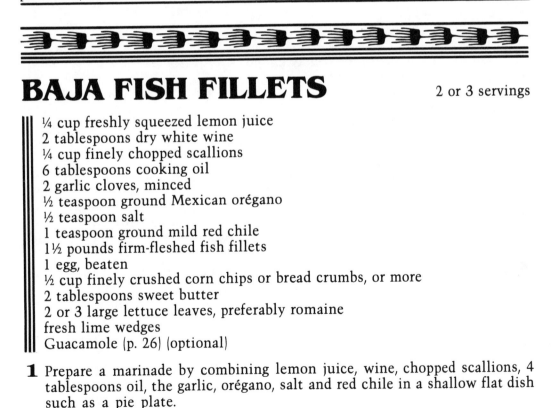

BAJA FISH FILLETS
2 or 3 servings

¼ cup freshly squeezed lemon juice
2 tablespoons dry white wine
¼ cup finely chopped scallions
6 tablespoons cooking oil
2 garlic cloves, minced
½ teaspoon ground Mexican orégano
½ teaspoon salt
1 teaspoon ground mild red chile
1½ pounds firm-fleshed fish fillets
1 egg, beaten
½ cup finely crushed corn chips or bread crumbs, or more
2 tablespoons sweet butter
2 or 3 large lettuce leaves, preferably romaine
fresh lime wedges
Guacamole (p. 26) (optional)

1 Prepare a marinade by combining lemon juice, wine, chopped scallions, 4 tablespoons oil, the garlic, orégano, salt and red chile in a shallow flat dish such as a pie plate.

2 Place fillets in the marinade and turn frequently, spooning the sauce over the fillets each time they are turned. Allow them to soak for 30 minutes to 1 hour.

3 Beat the egg in a shallow dish. Place the crumbs on a plate. Heat remaining oil and the butter in a large frying pan.

4 Dip each fillet into the egg and then coat evenly with the crumbs, pressing them in to make a uniform coating.

5 Fry until golden on each side. Serve on lettuce leaves with a dish of the reserved marinade, lime wedges and guacamole.

Note: *Any leftover marinade will keep in the refrigerator for several days. It is a very tasty sauce served with eggs.*

RED SNAPPER
VERA CRUZ STYLE

6 servings

¼ cup olive oil
6 good-size fresh red snapper fillets
1 teaspoon salt
1 medium-size white onion, finely chopped
2 large garlic cloves, minced
6 medium-size fresh tomatoes, peeled, chopped and seeded (about 2 cups)
juice of 1 fresh lime
½ teaspoon ground Mexican orégano
2 canned jalapeño chiles, seeded and cut into very fine strips
12 large pimiento-stuffed Spanish olives, sliced crosswise

1 Heat half of the oil in a large frying pan. Season the fillets with salt and fry until golden on each side. Remove to a warm plate and cover.

2 Add the rest of the oil to the pan and sauté the onion and garlic until they are translucent. Add the tomatoes, lime juice, orégano and chiles, and cook until flavors blend, about 10 minutes.

3 Reduce heat to a low simmer and place the fillets on top of the sauce. Spoon some of the sauce over the top of each fillet. Cover the pan and heat together for about 10 minutes. Taste the sauce and adjust the seasoning if desired.

4 Serve fish on warm plates with a mound of rice alongside. Spoon some sauce over each portion. Garnish with the sliced olives.

HERMOSILLO SNAPPER STUFFED WITH SHRIMPS
4 to 6 servings

This recipe is adapted from a dish I enjoyed in a little country hotel in Hermosillo, Mexico.

1 fresh red snapper, 3 to 4 pounds
⅓ pound fresh shrimps
¼ pound mushrooms
2 tablespoons butter
2 green onions, finely chopped
2 celery ribs, chopped
1 teaspoon minced fresh or ½ teaspoon dried tarragon
1 teaspoon minced fresh or ½ teaspoon dried basil
1 teaspoon minced fresh or ½ teaspoon dried savory
1 teaspoon minced fresh or ½ teaspoon dried thyme
salt and pepper
dry white wine
Snapper Sauce (recipe follows)

1 Rinse out red snapper and set aside. Shell shrimps and coarsely slice mushrooms.

2 Add shrimps and mushrooms to melted butter in a skillet. Add green onions, celery and herbs. Season to taste with salt and pepper. Sauté until shrimps are pink and mushrooms tender.

3 Stuff mixture into cavity of red snapper reserving about ¼ cup, then skewer closed. Place fish in a large roaster with a lid. Just before popping into a preheated 350°F. oven, drizzle with wine. Cover the pan. Baste fish frequently with wine in roaster as it bakes. Bake for about 30 minutes, or until done.

SNAPPER SAUCE

1 Prepare sauce in the same frying pan as you used for sautéing the stuffing. Remove the reserved shrimp and mushrooms to a small bowl and finely mince with a knife. Set aside.

2 Add 2 tablespoons butter to the pan and melt. Then add 1 chopped green onion, tops included, and sauté until clear. Add 2 tablespoons flour and stir until lightly browned.

3 Add 1 cup light cream and stir until thickened. Then add the minced reserved shrimp and mushroom mixture and stir to blend. Add a tablespoon of sherry, a pinch of thyme, ¼ teaspoon salt and some freshly ground black pepper.

4 When fish is done, remove to a heated platter. Add drippings from the bottom of the pan to the sauce and cook until it bubbles. Serve sauce separately.

COD IN ORANGE-LEMON SAUCE

4 servings

A tangy citrus sauce creates a fine warm-weather main dish on the light side, nice for summer evenings.

4 firm-fleshed fish fillets such as pompano, snapper or halibut
½ teaspoon salt
freshly ground black pepper
2 tablespoons minced fresh parsley
2 garlic cloves, crushed
¼ teaspoon ground comino
2 tablespoons olive oil
juice of ½ lemon
juice of 3 medium-size oranges

1 Sprinkle both sides of each fillet with salt and pepper. Place fillets in a large flat baking dish. Combine parsley, garlic, comino and oil and mix well. Pour half of the mixture over the fish, then turn fish over and drizzle remaining sauce over the second side.

2 Combine the orange and lemon juice and pour over all.

3 Cover and bake in a preheated 350°F. oven for 20 minutes, until the fish flakes easily with a fork. Serve hot.

PESCADO EN PECAN SALSA
Fish in Pecan Sauce

4 servings

1 cup dry white wine
½ cup water
1 bay leaf
½ teaspoon salt
4 whole peppercorns
2 pounds firm-fleshed white fish
1 small onion, sliced
1 garlic clove
½ cup shelled pecans
2 tablespoons fresh parsley sprigs
¼ teaspoon Spanish saffron
salt
pinch of ground mild red chile
juice of 1 lemon
4 lemon wedges

1 In a large frying pan, combine the wine, water, bay leaf, salt and peppercorns and bring to a boil. Simmer for about 10 minutes; remove the peppercorns and bay leaf.

2 Gently lower the fish into the simmering mixture. Continue to simmer for only a few minutes, until the flesh flakes easily with a fork.

3 Lift the fish out and place in a shallow ovenproof pan; cover. Place in 200°F. oven. Also place the dinner plates in the oven.

4 Pour the liquid from cooking the fish into a blender container. Add the onion, garlic, pecans, parsley and saffron. Blend until smooth. Taste and add salt, chile and lemon juice to taste. Heat until very warm, but do not boil.

5 Place a piece of fish on each heated plate and spoon sauce over the top. Garnish with a wedge of lemon.

CRUNCHY ALMOND SHRIMPS

3 or 4 servings

1 pound jumbo shrimps
2 eggs
¼ cup light cream
½ cup flour
1 garlic clove, crushed
1 cup crushed blanched almonds
cooking oil
fresh lime wedges

1 Shell and devein shrimps and split them butterfly fashion. Prepare a batter by beating the eggs, cream, flour and garlic together. Place almonds on a plate.

2 Dip each shrimp into the batter and then roll in the almonds to coat evenly. Set shrimps in a single layer on a large sheet of wax paper.

3 Heat oil in a deep frying pan to about 375°F.

4 Roll each shrimp again in the nuts and place in the hot oil. Fry until golden. Drain on absorbent paper toweling.

5 Serve hot with wedges of lime. Alongside serve steamed rice topped with scallions and a fresh fruit salad.

VEGETABLES & SIDE DISHES

The most traditional Tex-Mex side dishes are rice and beans. The rice is usually prepared with a touch of tomato, and the beans are either simply stewed or literally refried with cheese. Both provide a mild taste, complementing the spicy main dishes. Corn, potatoes and summer squash are the other vegetables most often served.

MEXICAN FRIED RICE

4 to 6 servings

2 cups chicken stock
1 teaspoon salt
¾ cup uncooked long-grain rice
3 tablespoons cooking oil
6 ounces Spanish-style tomato sauce or Bloody Mary mix
2 tablespoons chopped fresh green pepper
1 tablespoon minced onion

1 Bring the stock to a boil in a medium-size saucepan with a cover.

2 Add the salt and the rice, cover, and cook over medium heat for 15 minutes, or until done but not mushy.

3 Pour the oil into a heavy 10-inch frying pan and heat until hot. Add the rice and stir-fry for 10 minutes.

4 Add the rest of the ingredients and stir until well mixed. Cover and continue cooking for 10 minutes more, stirring occasionally.

Maximum Recommended Freezer Storage: *3 months*

MEXICAN HOT RICE
Chile-Flavored Rice

3 or 4 servings

½ cup uncooked rice
2 tablespoons lard or bacon drippings
1 large onion, finely chopped
4 large ripe tomatoes, chopped
4 cups chicken stock, boiling
½ teaspoon salt
3 tablespoons ground mild red chile, or hot chile for spicier flavor

1 Rinse the rice well with several washings of cold water.

2 Heat the lard or bacon drippings in a large heavy skillet. Add the rice and stir until it becomes brown. Add the onion and cook until it is golden.

3 Add the tomatoes, boiling stock, salt and chile. Add chile 1 tablespoon at a time, tasting after each addition. Add more salt if you prefer the rice saltier. Steam until rice is fluffy, about 15 minutes. After 15 minutes, check doneness and cook a bit more if needed.

ARROZ
Sweet Rice with Raisins and Almonds

4 servings

This sweet rice is a perfect complement to picadillo, mole and seafood specialties.

2¼ cups water
¾ teaspoon salt
¾ cup uncooked rice
1 teaspoon sugar
1 tablespoon butter
½ cup seedless raisins, coarsely chopped
½ cup blanched almonds, chopped

1 Pour the water into a saucepan with a close-fitting cover and bring to a vigorous boil. Add the salt and the rice and stir to distribute rice evenly. Cover and reduce heat to a simmer.

2 Cook without uncovering for about 15 minutes, or until rice is done. Rice should be tender and fluffy; if not, replace lid and continue cooking.

3 Add the sugar, butter, raisins and almonds, reserving about 1 tablespoon each of the raisins and almonds for garnish. Stir to distribute the ingredients evenly. Cover and allow to warm together for about 3 minutes.

4 Turn out on a serving dish or platter and garnish with the reserved raisins and almonds.

COMINO RICE
Cumin Rice

6 to 8 servings

2 tablespoons lard or butter
2 cups diced green or red bell pepper, 1 cup of each
1 medium-size onion, finely chopped
1 garlic clove, minced
1 teaspoon comino
1½ cups uncooked long-grain rice
1½ cups chicken stock, hot

1 Melt the lard or butter in a large kettle with a close-fitting cover.

2 Add the peppers and onion and cook until onion is wilted. Add the garlic, comino and rice, and stir until well mixed.

3 Add the hot stock and mix to distribute the rice evenly. Cover and steam for 15 minutes without disturbing. Then stir; if not as tender as desired, cook to desired doneness.

SOPA DE ARROZ CON GARBANZOS
Rice with Chick-Peas

4 to 6 servings

A Mexican version of Spanish rice which is good served with enchiladas, tacos, chiles rellenos, tamales or any of the typical Southwestern foods.

2 tablespoons bacon drippings
1 cup uncooked long-grain rice
1 medium-size onion, finely chopped
1 teaspoon salt
¼ teaspoon black pepper
2 garlic cloves, minced
1¼ cups canned tomatoes
2½ cups canned chick-peas, drained
water

1 Heat the drippings in a large heavy skillet over medium-high heat. Add the rice and brown it until rice is uniformly golden. Add the onion and sauté until onion is translucent.

2 Add the seasonings, garlic, tomatoes and chick-peas. Add enough water to cover the rice well.

3 Reduce the heat, cover, and simmer for about 30 minutes, or until rice is done. Do not stir while rice is cooking. If necessary, add additional liquid but do so carefully; pour the water against the side of the pan so as not to disturb the rice mixture. This trick assures fluffy Mexican rice and prevents gumminess.

Maximum Recommended Freezer Storage: *3 months*

GREEN CHILE CHEESE AND RICE BAKE

8 servings

A delicious low-cost, no-meat dish that has become quite popular recently in the Southwest. It can also be used as an accompaniment to other regional specialties such as chiles rellenos. Serve with fresh, warm tortillas or sopaipillas and a crisp salad.

8 ounces Monterey Jack cheese, sliced
2 cups sour cream
4 ounces canned chopped green chiles

4 cups cooked rice
salt and pepper
½ cup grated Cheddar cheese

1 Cut the Monterey Jack cheese into ½-inch strips. Mix the sour cream and green chiles together.

2 Alternate layers of rice, cheese and sour cream in a buttered 2-quart casserole. Bake at 350°F. for 30 minutes.

3 After 15 minutes of baking, sprinkle the top of the casserole with the grated Cheddar. Bake until Cheddar is melted and golden. Serve hot.

Maximum Recommended Freezer Storage: *2 months*

FRIJOLES
Stewed Pinto Beans

3½ cups

Frijoles are a staple in the Tex-Mex diet. Many families have them at least twice, often three times, a day. The spotted pinto bean is the most popular for this. They cook to a light brown color and develop a wonderful rich flavor when cooked slowly for a long time. The beans should be soft when done. Serve as is or refried, or in any number of casserole or combination dishes. A favorite Rio Grande tradition is to serve the beans with a green or red chile meat sauce for topping. Sopaipillas or tortillas complete the meal.

2 cups dried pinto beans
5 cups water, or more
1 teaspoon sugar
1 garlic clove, minced (optional)
1½ teaspoons salt, or more
½ cup small cubes of salt pork, or 3 tablespoons bacon drippings

1 Wash beans and soak overnight. Discard soaking water. Add the 5 cups fresh water and the sugar and simmer for 30 minutes.

2 Add garlic and salt and simmer for at least 3 hours. Add more water as needed.

3 Add salt pork or drippings and simmer for another 30 minutes before serving. Adjust seasoning if necessary.

Maximum Recommended Freezer Storage: *1 year*

FRIJOLES REFRITOS
Refried Beans   6 to 8 servings

This most popular of all side dishes is served from Arizona to Texas and New Mexico to California.

3 to 4 tablespoons bacon drippings
4 cups cooked pinto beans
2 garlic cloves, crushed
salt, if needed
¾ cup grated Monterey Jack or Cheddar cheese

1 Heat the bacon drippings or lard in a heavy skillet over low heat. Add the beans and a little liquid and mash them, using a masher or the back of a spatula, until they are thoroughly crushed. Add garlic, and salt if needed.

2 Switch heat to medium and cook for 20 to 30 minutes, until the beans are thoroughly heated and edges are somewhat crispy.

3 Serve piping hot, garnished with the cheese.

Note: *These beans may be used for a stuffing for burritos, tacos or sopaipillas.*

Maximum Recommended Freezer Storage: *2 months*

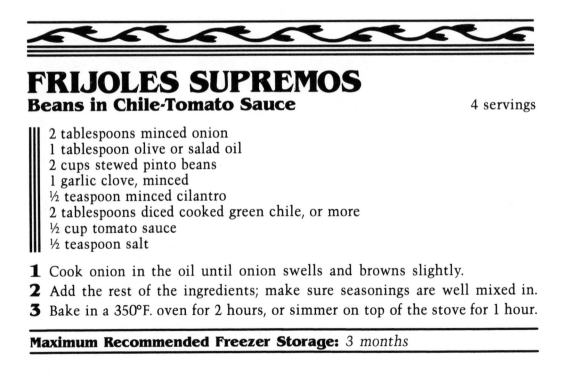

FRIJOLES SUPREMOS
Beans in Chile-Tomato Sauce   4 servings

2 tablespoons minced onion
1 tablespoon olive or salad oil
2 cups stewed pinto beans
1 garlic clove, minced
½ teaspoon minced cilantro
2 tablespoons diced cooked green chile, or more
½ cup tomato sauce
½ teaspoon salt

1 Cook onion in the oil until onion swells and browns slightly.

2 Add the rest of the ingredients; make sure seasonings are well mixed in.

3 Bake in a 350°F. oven for 2 hours, or simmer on top of the stove for 1 hour.

Maximum Recommended Freezer Storage: *3 months*

CALABACITAS
New Mexican-Style Zucchini

8 servings

Calabacitas can be served as a side or main dish.

4 tablespoons butter
2 pounds lean round steak, cut into 1-inch cubes
5 medium-size zucchini
3 ears of fresh corn, cut from the cob, or 2 cups whole-kernel corn, drained
½ cup chopped green chiles
2 garlic cloves, minced
2 teaspoons salt
dash of Mexican orégano
¼ teaspoon comino
¾ cup grated Cheddar cheese

1 Melt butter in a large frying pan over medium heat. Add round steak cubes and brown on all sides.

2 Slice zucchini into thin rounds and fry in the same pan until slightly tender, about 10 minutes.

3 Add corn kernels, green chiles, garlic, salt and herbs, and cook together for about 10 minutes.

4 Add grated cheese and stir until it is melted. Serve at once.

Maximum Recommended Freezer Storage: *8 months*

CALABACITAS GUISADAS
Squash in Spicy Sauce

4 servings

6 small zucchini
2 large tomatoes, peeled and finely chopped
1 large onion, finely chopped
½ teaspoon minced cilantro
½ cup chopped green chiles (optional)
salt
1 cup Monterey Jack cheese, grated

1 Slice the zucchini. Combine with the tomatoes, onion, cilantro and green chiles. Cook over medium-low heat for 30 to 45 minutes, or until squash is tender. Add salt to taste.

2 Add the cheese and stir into the vegetables.

Variation: *Add 1 cup sour cream on top of the vegetables before serving.*
Maximum Recommended Freezer Storage: *8 months*

QUELITES
Steamed Greens

4 to 6 servings

1½ pounds fresh spinach
3 tablespoons chopped onion
1 tablespoon bacon drippings
¼ teaspoon ground red chile
1 teaspoon salt

1 Wash spinach and remove stem ends. Steam in a medium-size saucepan for 10 minutes. Drain and chop.

2 Sauté chopped onion in fat in a large skillet. Add spinach, chile and salt. Mix together. Cook for an additional 5 minutes.

Maximum Recommended Freezer Storage: *8 months*

CHEESY BROILED TOMATO HALVES

4 servings

This recipe is not Mexican, but it makes a light complement to any hearty Mexican meal.

2 medium-size to large firm tomatoes
2 tablespoons butter
1 teaspoon seasoned salt
freshly ground black pepper
4 tablespoons grated Parmesan cheese
2 tablespoons bread crumbs, toasted
4 teaspoons snipped chives

1 Rinse tomatoes, then cut into halves. Place them, cut sides up, on a baking pan.

2 Cut butter into small dots and distribute evenly over the tomatoes. Season with salt and pepper, dividing salt among the 4 tomato halves.

3 Sprinkle on remaining ingredients in the order listed, distributing them evenly among the 4 halves.

4 Place under a preheated broiler for about 15 minutes, or until cheese melts and tomatoes are thoroughly heated.

Not Recommended for Freezing

INDIAN-STYLE CORN ON THE COB

Roasting corn as the Indians have done for centuries is made to order for patio suppers and picnics. Serve with grilled hamburgers, steaks or Tex-Mex specialties.

1 gallon cool water
1 tablespoon salt
freshly picked corn with husks and silks intact

1 Pour the water into a clean sink or large kettle and mix in the salt. Add corn and soak for 10 minutes.

2 Place corn on the grill 4 to 5 inches above the coals, or toss into a medium hot campfire, being sure to place directly on the coals. Turn frequently. Corn will be done in 12 to 15 minutes.

3 The best way to test for doneness is to peel back a very small section of the husk at the base of the largest ear. If the kernels when pierced do not yield a milky substance, corn is done.

Not Recommended for Freezing

CHILE CORN   4 servings

2 tablespoons butter
2 cups fresh sweet corn kernels cut from cobs
2 green chiles, coarsely chopped
1 small garlic clove, minced
½ teaspoon salt
dash of freshly ground black pepper

1 Heat the butter in a frying pan and add the corn, chiles and seasoning.

2 Cover and cook until the corn is tender, about 12 minutes. If corn seems dry, add a few drops of water.

Maximum Recommended Freezer Storage: *8 months*

NEW MEXICAN CORN CUSTARD

10 to 12 generous servings

This corn custard is the best I have ever tasted. The dish is especially nice to serve with any buffet featuring roast meat.

4 eggs, beaten
8 cups yellow or white cream-style corn
1½ cups yellow or white cornmeal, or cracker or tostado crumbs
1½ teaspoons salt
1 garlic clove, minced
1 teaspoon baking powder
¾ cup melted butter
8 ounces canned chopped green chiles
¾ pound sharp Cheddar cheese, grated

1 Preheat oven to 375°F. Combine all of the ingredients in the order listed and pour into a buttered 3-quart casserole.

2 Bake in the oven for 45 minutes, then reduce the temperature to 325°F. and continue to bake for 15 to 45 minutes. Or keep the casserole in a 150°F. oven for several hours awaiting serving time.

Note: *If you have a blender or food processor, put the ingredients, part at a time, into the machine and process until mixed. Cheese will not need grating before blending; simply cut it into chunks.*

Maximum Recommended Freezer Storage: *8 months*

ELOTE
Mexican-Style Corn Custard

4 servings

A mild sweet flavor to accompany any rich or spicy meat dish.

3 ears of fresh corn, cut off the cob, or ¾ cup frozen corn
1 cup cream
1 teaspoon baking powder
1 teaspoon salt
dash of black pepper
1 tablespoon sugar
3 eggs

1 Put all ingredients in a blender container. Whirl until the ingredients are well blended. Lacking a blender, whip the cream, seasonings and eggs together and combine with the corn.

2 Butter a 1-quart baking dish, add the custard, and bake in a 350°F. oven for 40 to 60 minutes, or until a knife inserted near the center comes out clean.

Maximum Recommended Freezer Storage: *1 year*

MEXICAN HOMINY

4 to 6 servings

Mexican hominy tastes similar to posole when prepared in this manner. You can serve it as a side dish; or add a pound of browned sausage to it when adding the cheese and serve it as a main dish.

2 tablespoons bacon drippings
18 ounces, or 2½ cups, canned golden hominy, well drained
1 medium-size onion, chopped
1¼ cups canned tomatoes
1 cup Red Chile Sauce (p. 44)
salt
½ pound Monterey Jack or Cheddar cheese, grated

1 Melt the bacon drippings in a large skillet and add the drained hominy and onion.

2 Sauté for 6 to 8 minutes. Add the tomatoes and allow to cook until the mixture no longer looks watery.

3 Add the chile sauce and stir well. Season with salt to taste. Just before serving, stir in the cheese and cook until it melts.

Variation: *The dish, except for the cheese, can be prepared in advance and placed in a well-greased casserole. Just before serving top it with the cheese and place in a hot oven until warm.*

Maximum Recommended Freezer Storage: *8 months, without cheese; 3 months, with cheese added*

PAPAS Y CHILE
Potatoes and Chile
6 servings

This popular vegetable combination goes well with any meat dish.

2 tablespoons bacon drippings
2 onions, finely chopped
4 medium-size potatoes, cooked and diced
2 teaspoons salt
1 cup chopped mild green chiles

1 In a large heavy skillet, heat the bacon drippings and sauté the onions until translucent. Add the potatoes and fry until golden, stirring often.

2 Add more bacon drippings if needed to keep from sticking. Sprinkle with salt. Stir in green chiles and cover. Allow flavors to mingle for 3 to 5 minutes, stirring a time or two.

Not Recommended for Freezing

CHORIZO PAPAS
Sausage and Potatoes
4 servings

High up in the hills, the sizzle and spicy aroma of chorizo papas really "stirs up an appetite." Until some camping buddies prepared these for me, I only had experience with savory chorizo eggs. They are good any time but especially good for a hearty breakfast.

4 chorizo sausages, or 1 pound bulk Chorizo (p. 130)
3 large or 4 medium-size potatoes
1 teaspoon salt

1 Remove casings from sausages and coarsely chop the meat into a large well-seasoned or buttered skillet. Heat over medium heat, stirring and chopping to make a crumbled mixture. Peel and slice potatoes. (Often I do not peel them.)

2 After sausage is crumbly and has rendered some fat, add the potato slices and salt. Stir and cook until the potatoes have become rosy red and tender.

Variation: *If a crisper potato is preferred, cook the potato slices in shortening until lightly browned and cook chorizo separately. Combine and cook together with the lid on for about 10 minutes.*

Not Recommended for Freezing

GARBANZOS
Stewed Chick-Peas

A substitute for frijoles or rice to accompany any meat dish.

1 cup dried chick-peas
water
1 teaspoon salt
1 onion, chopped
small chunk of salt pork
2 tablespoons bacon drippings
¼ cup ground red chile
pinch of comino
pinch of Mexican orégano
pinch of cilantro

1 Soak the chick-peas in water overnight. Drain, discard soaking water and add fresh water to cover. Add the salt and bring to a boil. Simmer until tender, 1 to 2 hours.

2 When the chick-peas are tender, fry the onion and salt pork in the bacon drippings in a small frying pan until onion is translucent.

3 Add onion, salt pork, chile and seasonings to the chick-peas and simmer together slightly before serving.

Maximum Recommended Freezer Storage: *3 months*

DESSERTS

Most Tex-Mex meals end with simple desserts to top off the rich spiciness of the main dishes. The two most popular traditional choices are fruits and custards prepared various ways. As a texture and flavor contrast, cookies are frequently served alongside.

Fresh fruit assortments of most any combination are excellent. Favorites are mango slices generously drizzled with fresh lime juice and garnished with pomegranate seeds, blueberries or other berries. Guava jelly bar candy available in Mexican and Southwestern delicacy shops is excellent cut into rectangles and served with chunks of Monterey Jack cheese. Melon mélanges made with at least three types such as watermelon, honeydew and cantaloupe are popular and great if marinated in some rum or tequila.

Serve sherbet or ice cream with a splash of Kahlúa on it for a simple hot-weather dessert.

BIZCOCHITOS
Spicy Cookies
5 dozen

The most popular Southwestern cookies are rich, crisp, spicy and easy to make. Bizcochitos are popular for serving at coffees, teas and during the Christmas holidays. For a wonderful treat, serve with steaming mugs of New Mexican Chocolate (p. 40).

6 cups sifted flour
3 teaspoons baking powder
1 teaspoon salt
1 pound lard or butter (lard is traditional and makes more tender cookies)
1¾ cups sugar
2 teaspoons aniseeds
2 eggs
¼ cup brandy, or more
1 tablespoon ground cinnamon

1 Preheat oven to 350°F.

2 Sift flour with baking powder and salt.

3 Cream lard with 1½ cups sugar and aniseeds by hand or with an electric mixer at medium speed. Beat eggs until light and fluffy; add to the creamed mixture. Add flour mixture and brandy and mix well until blended. Use only enough brandy to form a stiff dough.

4 Knead dough lightly and pat or roll to ¼- to ½-inch thickness. Cut into fancy shapes. The fleur-de-lis shape is traditional for these cookies.

5 Dust tops of cookies with a mixture of ¼ cup sugar and the cinnamon. Bake for 10 minutes, or until very lightly browned.

Freezing Hint: *Place cookies in a rigid container, separating the layers of cookies with sheets of wax paper, foil or clear plastic wrap.*
Maximum Recommended Freezer Storage: *6 months*

BUÑUELOS
Sopaipillas in Syrup
4 dozen

In the old days, buñuelos were a popular afternoon tea treat, but because they take quite a bit of time to prepare you seldom find them served. I think you will find them worth the trouble, especially for a special occasion.

1 Prepare the recipe for Sopaipillas (p. 53), only cut the dough into rounds instead of squares. After deep-frying them, soak in the following syrup. Serve warm. Or serve the warm sopaipillas with the warm sauce for dunking.

||| 6 tablespoons light brown sugar
½ cup hot water
½ cup light sherry
½ cup seedless dark raisins
1 teaspoon ground cinnamon
⅛ teaspoon maple flavoring (optional)

2 Combine all the ingredients in a saucepan and boil until slightly thickened.

Not Recommended for Freezing

BUÑUELOS MEXICO CITY STYLE
Deep-Fried Cookies 3 to 6 dozen, depending on the size of rosette iron

These delicate cookies resemble Swedish rosette cookies and are surprisingly easy to make. They are very different from the other buñuelos and add variety to any cookie assortment.

||| 1 egg
2 cups water
2½ cups flour
oil for frying
½ cup sugar
2 tablespoons ground cinnamon

1 Be sure you have a rosette iron or other cookie iron. Using an electric blender, place the egg, water and flour in that order in the blender container. Blend at a high speed until the mixture looks like cream.

2 Heat the oil to 375°F.

3 Heat the cookie iron in the oil. Quickly dip the hot iron into the batter only up to the top of the iron; do not submerge the iron.

4 At once lower the batter-covered iron into the hot oil until the cookie slips off the iron. Repeat, frying only a few at a time for 2 to 3 minutes each.

5 Remove the cookies from the hot oil as soon as they are a light golden color. Drain, then sprinkle with sugar-cinnamon mixture. Store in rigid containers.

Variation: *Dust cookies with powdered sugar. I like to prepare half each way.*
Freezing Hint: *See Bizcochitos (p. 164)*
Maximum Recommended Freezer Storage: *6 months*

NEW MEXICAN PRALINES

4 dozen

Pralines make a wonderful dessert following Mexican food. They are great for buffets when individually wrapped in colorful tissue paper and tied with jumbo yarn. For holidays and parties, I've often tied them to a piñon tree encircling the patio or to a branch of a cedar I used for the centerpiece.

1 cup firmly packed brown sugar
2 cups granulated sugar
3 tablespoons light corn syrup
¼ teaspoon salt
1 cup light cream
4 tablespoons butter
2 teaspoons maple flavoring
1½ cups shelled pecan halves

1 Butter a heavy 3-quart saucepan on the inside.

2 Combine sugars, syrup, salt, cream and butter in the saucepan and stir until well blended.

3 Cook slowly over medium heat until candy reaches the medium firm-ball stage (246°F.). Remove from heat.

4 Let candy stand undisturbed for a few minutes. Then add flavoring and pecans and beat a few whips until creamy.

5 Drop by spoonfuls onto wax paper. If candy begins to harden, add a few drops of light cream; place over the lowest heat of the range and stir until creamy; it should drop smoothly from the spoon.

Variation: *Milk or evaporated milk may be used instead of cream. If milk is substituted, use about 1 tablespoon more butter.*

Freezing Hint: *Place in rigid container, separating layers of candies with sheets of wax paper.*

Maximum Recommended Freezer Storage: *1 year*

SANTA FE SUNDAES
Spicy Hot Fudge Sundae

6 servings

4 ounces (4 squares) Mexican chocolate
1 cup light cream
ice cream

1 In a heavy small saucepan set over low temperature, melt the Mexican chocolate. Add the cream, a few drops at a time, stirring to mix evenly. Let mixture heat until the chocolate is thoroughly melted.

2 Serve warm over ice cream. Sauce keeps in the refrigerator for 2 months.

Variation: *If Mexican chocolate is not available, prepare your favorite chocolate or fudge sauce, adding about ½ teaspoon each of ground cinnamon, nutmeg and cloves.*

FLAMING PUMPKIN FLAN 10 to 12 servings

1¼ cups sugar
3 cups evaporated milk or scalded thin cream
2 cups pumpkin purée
⅔ cup sugar
½ cup rum
6 whole eggs
2 extra egg yolks
1 teaspoon salt
1 teaspoon ground cinnamon
¼ teaspoon ground ginger
½ teaspoon ground nutmeg
½ teaspoon ground mace
1 cup whipping cream
¼ to ½ cup brandy (optional)

1 Spoon the sugar into a heavy skillet set over medium heat. Slowly melt the sugar, stirring constantly until it becomes a smooth syrup and deep amber in color.

2 Pour the sugar into a well-chilled, buttered round 2-quart glass casserole. Tip to coat sides and bottom of the casserole with the caramel; chill.

3 Prepare custard by mixing together all remaining ingredients except the whipping cream and the brandy. Pour into the caramel-lined casserole.

4 Set casserole in a pan of hot water and bake in a 350°F. oven for about 1¼ hours, or until set. Meanwhile, whip the cream.

5 Cool custard at room temperature for 10 minutes, then invert on a serving plate and lift off the casserole. Wait about 20 minutes more before serving.

6 Heat the brandy (or use more rum) until it becomes hot but does not boil. Pour immediately over the flan and ignite; rush to the dinner table. Serve with dollops of whipped cream.

Not Recommended for Freezing

NATILLAS
Soft Custard
6 to 8 servings

This soft fluffy custard is delicious after a hot spicy meal.

1 quart milk
¾ cup sugar
⅛ teaspoon salt
4 eggs, separated
¼ cup flour
1½ teaspoons freshly grated nutmeg

1 Pour the milk into a heavy saucepan and add the sugar and salt. Scald over medium-low heat.

2 Make a paste with the egg yolks, flour and 1 cup of the scalded milk.

3 Add this thickening to the rest of the scalded milk and continue to cook until mixture reaches the consistency of soft custard.

4 Beat the egg whites until stiff but not dry, and fold them into the custard.

5 Spoon custard into individual dishes. Top with nutmeg and refrigerate until ready to serve.

Variations: *Natillas con fruta fresca: serve the natillas over fresh fruits such as pineapple, orange sections with membranes removed, peaches or other desired fruit. This makes an attractive dessert, especially when served in sherbet glasses.*

Not Recommended for Freezing

FLAN CARAMELISADO
Custard with Caramel Topping
6 servings

Flan is a delicately flavored caramel custard and one of the most traditional desserts.

1½ cups sugar
6 eggs
3½ cups milk
1 cinnamon stick
1 teaspoon vanilla extract

1. Caramelize ½ cup sugar in a large skillet over medium heat, stirring constantly until sugar is melted and browned. Pour immediately into the bottoms of 6 buttered custard cups.
2. Beat eggs until foamy. Gradually add the remaining cup of sugar, beating well after each addition.
3. Heat the milk with the cinnamon stick over medium-high heat to just below boiling. Add milk to egg mixture, stirring until sugar is dissolved.
4. Strain egg mixture for a very smooth texture and add vanilla.
5. Pour into the caramel-lined custard cups. Set cups in a pan of hot water and bake in a 350°F. oven for 1 hour and 10 minutes, or until a knife inserted comes out clean. Serve warm or chilled.

Not Recommended for Freezing

FLAN VIRGINIA
Custard with Caramel Nut Topping
4 to 6 servings

A luscious, velvety smooth custard served in the true Southwestern manner. This recipe was concocted by my Aunt Virginia.

½ cup sugar
1 cup coarsely chopped pecans
15 ounces sweetened condensed milk
15 ounces regular milk
6 eggs
1 teaspoon vanilla extract

1. Caramelize the sugar in a heavy skillet. Transfer while hot to the bottom of a buttered 1½-quart casserole or mold, or to 4 to 6 individual baking dishes.
2. Sprinkle the pecans on top of the caramelized sugar.
3. Blend remaining ingredients together in an electric blender; or whip the eggs first, then add both kinds of milk and the vanilla. Pour gently into the prepared mold or dishes. Set the baking dish or dishes in a shallow layer of water in another pan.
4. Bake at 350°F. for about 1 hour, until firm, or until a knife inserted in the center comes out clean. Serve warm or cold.

Variation: *Serve with a dollop of whipped cream.*

Not Recommended for Freezing

MEXICAN WEDDING CAKES
4 dozen

These rich, buttery cookies are a nice addition to a tea cookie assortment and as an accompaniment to ice cream.

> 2 cups sifted flour
> ¼ cup sugar
> ½ teaspoon salt
> ½ pound butter
> 2 teaspoons vanilla extract
> 2 cups finely chopped nuts, preferably pecans
> confectioners' sugar

1 Preheat oven to 325°F.

2 Sift together flour, sugar and salt.

3 Mix butter into the dry ingredients in a large bowl. Add the vanilla and nuts and mix well.

4 Shape dough into ½-inch balls or into small crescent shapes.

5 Place 1 inch apart on a lightly greased baking sheet. Bake for about 20 minutes, or until lightly browned. While still warm, roll in confectioners' sugar.

Variation: *Decorate with powdered sugar frosting.*
Maximum Recommended Freezer Storage: *8 months*

MINCEMEAT EMPANADAS
Fried Pies
6 dozen large or 9 dozen small pies

Holidays and festivals are not complete in the Rio Grande area of New Mexico without empanadas. There are hundreds of ways to make these fried pies or turnovers. This is my favorite.

DOUGH

> 1 teaspoon dry yeast
> ½ cup lukewarm water, or more (105° to 115°F.)
> ¼ cup shortening
> 4 cups flour
> 1 teaspoon salt
> 1 tablespoon sugar

1 Dissolve yeast in water; set aside.

2 Cut shortening into all dry ingredients.

3 Mix the dissolved yeast and water with the dry ingredients until you have a stiff dough. More water may be needed.

4 Do not let the dough rise, but roll it out to a thin sheet. Cut with a round biscuit or larger cutter, depending upon the size of empanadas preferred.

5 Place a small mound of cool Mincemeat Filling (recipe follows) in the center of the dough. Moisten half of the edge of the dough and fold over to make a half-moon shape. Tightly seal the pastry, using your favorite edging or a fork dipped into flour. Tex-Mex cooks make an edging called *repulgar*, which is a scalloped edging made by flipping each piece of dough over the thumb by the forefingers and twisting to make a very tight seal.

6 Deep-fry the pies in oil heated to 420°F. An electric deep-fryer works best. Fry only a few pies at a time until they are golden on the first side. Then turn and fry until golden on the second side, about 3 minutes. Drain on absorbent paper.

7 Dust with powdered sugar if desired. Serve warm with a topping of whipped cream or ice cream.

MINCEMEAT FILLING

enough for 6 dozen large
or 9 dozen small pies

1½ pounds boiling meat (beef or pork tongue can be used for part of the meat)
1 cup raisins
1 cup applesauce
¾ cup sugar
½ cup dark syrup or light molasses
½ teaspoon crushed coriander seed
4 teaspoons cloves (use less for milder flavor)
1 teaspoon salt
4 cups piñóns, shelled walnuts or almonds
¼ cup dry sherry or brandy

1 Simmer the meat in water to cover until tender. Grind or purée in an electric blender.

2 Add remaining ingredients and mix well. The filling should be thick and moist.

3 If it seems dry, add more liquid. Let it rest for several hours to blend flavors, then use for filling.

Freezing Hint: *Place in a rigid container.*
Maximum Recommended Freezer Storage: *4 months*

SOUTHWESTERN PUMPKIN PIE

6 to 8 servings

Rum in the filling complemented by a crunchy praline topping makes a luscious and different pumpkin pie.

2 eggs
2 cups pumpkin purée
¾ cup brown sugar
½ teaspoon salt
1 teaspoon ground cinnamon
½ teaspoon ground allspice
½ teaspoon ground nutmeg
½ teaspoon ground ginger
⅛ teaspoon ground cloves
⅛ teaspoon ground mace
½ cup dark rum
pastry for 1-crust 9-inch pie
4 tablespoons butter
¾ cup granulated sugar
1 cup coarsely chopped pecans
1 cup whipping cream
2 tablespoons rum

1 Place eggs, pumpkin, brown sugar, salt and all the spices in the container of an electric blender. Blend at high speed for about 30 seconds. Add the rum for the last few seconds. Or use a mixer to combine all these ingredients.

2 Line a 9-inch pie dish with the pastry. Pour the pumpkin into the dish.

3 Bake at 450°F. for 10 minutes; reduce heat to 350°F. and continue to bake for 30 to 40 minutes. Pie is done when a silver knife inserted in the center comes out clean.

4 Meanwhile prepare the praline crunch topping; melt the butter in a small skillet. Stir in ½ cup granulated sugar and add the pecans.

5 Cook over moderate heat, stirring constantly, until the sugar begins to turn golden.

6 Remove from heat and turn onto a buttered plate until the praline hardens. Crumble.

7 Mix whipping cream with rum and remaining ¼ cup granulated sugar. Whip until almost stiff. Cut pie into servings, spoon some cream on each piece, and serve the crumbled praline on the cream.

Not Recommended for Freezing

FRUIT EMPANADAS

3 dozen large or
4½ dozen small pies

Empanadas can be baked or fried. For frying, a bread-type dough is used; for baking, a richer pastry dough is used. Usually, the baked ones are filled with a dried fruit filling. Apricot-filled ones have long been favorites, especially when served warm and topped with rich vanilla ice cream.

PASTRY

2 cups flour
1 teaspoon baking powder
½ teaspoon salt
⅛ teaspoon ground coriander seed (optional)
½ cup shortening
⅓ cup milk

1 Sift flour, measure, then mix with remaining dry ingredients.

2 Cut in shortening and mix until you have the consistency of coarse meal.

3 Add milk, a few drops at a time, and mix until the dough will form a ball; use only enough milk to make a pastry. Allow to set for a few minutes.

4 Preheat oven to 450°F. Roll dough out to a thin sheet and cut into rounds of desired size. Place a spoonful of filling on the center of each. Moisten the edge lightly and firmly press the edges together, using preferred edging (see Mincemeat Empanadas, p. 170).

5 Place filled empanadas on a dry baking sheet and bake at 450°F. for 10 to 12 minutes, or until golden.

FRUIT FILLING

enough for 3 dozen large or 4½ dozen small pies

½ pound dried peaches or apricots
1¼ cups sugar
¼ teaspoon salt
1 teaspoon ground cinnamon
½ teaspoon ground nutmeg
½ cup raisins, soaked in warm water

1 Soak peaches or apricots in hot water to cover until soft, about 30 minutes.

2 Simmer peaches in a small quantity of water over medium high heat until they are very soft. Drain fruit and cool, then mash or purée in an electric blender.

3 Add remaining ingredients and mix well. Use to fill empanadas.

Freezing Hint: *Place in rigid container.*

Maximum Recommended Freezer Storage: *8 months*

ORANGES MEXICANO

4 to 6 servings

A refreshingly light dessert, perfect following a hearty Mexican meal.

3 seedless oranges
2 tablespoons powdered sugar
2 tablespoons freshly squeezed lime juice, or more
1 jigger of tequila (1½ ounces)
½ jigger of Cointreau or Triple Sec (¾ ounce)

1 Peel oranges and cut into rounds if membranes are tender, or section them and remove membranes if tough. (Canned mandarins may be substituted.) Sprinkle the orange pieces with the sugar. (Omit sugar if using mandarins.)

2 Squeeze lime juice over all and gently mix until all pieces are well coated. Macerate in the refrigerator.

3 Just before serving, add the liqueurs and stir together. Serve in stemmed glasses.

Not Recommended for Freezing

MENUS

Tex-Mex meals have much to recommend them—exciting flavors ranging from mild through exotic to spicy, bright color combinations, easy preparation, and they are also less expensive than most other types of cooking. Tex-Mex foods evolved in the border states as an answer to the need for hearty foods to serve several hungry "hands" as they moved about the vast West.

Menus are innovative—the mere serving of these sumptuous foods makes a meal an event. While there are some traditional go-togethers, you can still be artistic and creative in developing menu and decorating themes: I've found adding a few Mexican touches to the table setting, room decorations or my hostess dress—even a bright sash swishing to the floor from your waist can do a lot—makes the occasion much more festive and at very little or no cost.

For special parties, get some good mariachi (Mexican street band) music for atmosphere, and tip off your guests—they might like to dress Mexican, too.

To set the appropriate mood, decorations of paper piñatas and flowers in brilliant shades can be purchased inexpensively or you can make them yourself. They last a long time if not exposed to bright sunlight. The flowers are especially effective tied to plants or trees, or tied to the porch and elsewhere on the outside of the house. Bright-colored candles add a festive air when placed in tin or glass holders.

For table decorations that will also contribute to this mood use rustic-looking pottery, painted enamelware, colorful serving pieces—if you have none of these use gaily colored napkins, placemats or tablecloths. Baskets, tinware, decorative Mexican items, even a sombrero can be used for an authentic-looking centerpiece. Another sure hit for parties is to create a guacamole and tostado server from a sombrero—just bash in the crown to hold the bowl of guacamole and then scatter the tostados around the brim. A fringed serape or Mexican shawl can be used as a table drape under the centerpiece or can extend down the sides for buffets.

All of the following menus are amazingly adaptable to both entertaining and for family meals. Many of these menus can be planned so that some of the dishes can be prepared ahead to make for smooth sailing at serving time.

To give yourself the greatest flexibility and enjoyment, periodically check your freezer and keep an up-to-date shopping list to make certain you always have on hand the basics for your own special Tex-Mex meals. Standbys such as tortillas, tamales, grated cheese, basic sauces, chile stews, fresh pure seasonings and red and green chiles in your freezer allow for abundant variety on a moment's notice.

BRUNCH

Bloody Marias *(p. 36)*
Huevos Rancheros *(p. 78)*
Bolillos or Wheat-Flour Tortillas *(p. 58 and p. 52)*
sweet butter
jam
Hot Mexican Coffee or New Mexican Chocolate *(p. 40)*

All the foods can be prepared either a day or a few hours ahead of time, making this menu convenient for the host and/or hostess. For surprisingly great Marias, use large tulip- or bulbous-shaped stemmed glasses, rimmed with salt and frozen a few hours before the party. Just before guests arrive or before you're ready to sip your Maria, place pottery plates in the oven set at low (200°F.). Wrap the rolls or tortillas in foil and heat at the same time. Warm the sauce. Just before serving, poach the eggs, cover with the sauce, and serve. An alternative menu could feature Sante Fe omelets.

LUNCHEON AL FRESCO

In the heat of summer, I've found this menu to be one of the best. It is perfect served on a shaded patio under a bright blue sky.

White Sangria *(p. 38)*
Tostados Compuestas *(p. 68)*
Salsa Colorado *(p. 43)*
Natillas with Fresh Peaches *(p. 168)*
Tostados *(p. 32)*

Several hours before the luncheon, prepare the sangria, the filling ingredients, the salsa, tostados and natillas. Just before serving, assemble the tostados. Prepare the peaches and place them in a citric-acid preparation to prevent darkening. Excellent alternative main dishes are chalupas, chicken or guacamole-filled tacos or flautas.

TRADITIONAL TEX-MEX DINNER

An authentic menu found at only the finest restaurants and homes throughout the border states. In the summer I prefer to enjoy the season's bounty—green chiles—while in the fall and spring red chile seems best.

Frozen Peachy Daiquiris *(p. 37)*
Guacamole *(p. 26)* **with tostados and fresh vegetable dunkers**
Tostados *(p. 32)*
Salsa *(any is good; see pp. 42 to 43)*
Green Chile Enchiladas *(p. 88)*
Chiles Rellenos with Red Chile Sauce *(pp. 110, 44)*
Mexican Fried Rice *(p. 150)*
Sopaipillas *(p. 53)*
honey
Fruit Empanadas *(p. 173)* **with homemade or**
rich French vanilla ice cream

Ahead of time, prepare the tostados, salsa, enchiladas or chiles rellenos sauce and grate the cheese, chop the onion, and fry the tortillas for enchiladas, or prepare chiles and stuff them if making rellenos. Bake the empanadas; if desired, these can be prepared ahead and even frozen. An hour before, assemble daiquiri ingredients in blender and prepare the guacamole. Measure the ingredients for the rice and sopaipillas. Pour the oil into a deep-fryer or heavy deep frying pan or Dutch oven. Just before guests arrive, prepare daiquiris, start the rice, and prepare the batter if making chiles rellenos. Prepare the sopaipilla dough, knead it, and set aside. If you don't wish to make the sopaipillas while guests are on hand, they can be fried ahead, but they definitely suffer; the same is true for chiles rellenos.

I have found that guests really like to watch and even participate in making chiles rellenos and sopaipillas. They like to see the action and learn the tricks for making them.

MERIENDA

A delightful Southwestern custom stemming from Spain is to serve a merienda, *the Spanish version of the continental tea service. While living in New Mexico and actively involved in numerous benefits and open houses, I always found a* merienda *very well received. If possible have your* merienda *outdoors and decorate with lots of oversize paper flowers, hang tissue-wrapped pralines from yarn bows on the trees and string up many generous oversized* ristras *(strings of dried red chiles).*

fresh fruit
Monterey Jack cheese
Buñuelos *(p. 164)*
Minted Tea
Pralines *(p. 166)*
Bizcochitos *(p. 164)*
Mexican Coffee or New Mexican Chocolate *(p. 40)*

Bake the cookies a day or two ahead. An hour or so before the *merienda* arrange artfully cut fresh fruit pieces of various colors and types on fresh grape or other tree leaves. Set the cheese on a cutting board and prepare the beverages. Serve buffet style.

EL PASO BARBECUE

A truly western dinner meant to be served only under the stars.

Squeezins *(p. 39)*
Chile Nuts *(p. 31)*
Mexican Spareribs *(p. 128)*
Calabacitas *(p. 155)*
Southwestern Corn Bread *(p. 57)*
Pickled Coleslaw *(p. 69)*
Oranges Mexicano *(p. 174)*
coffee

A day ahead, prepare the chile nuts, marinate the spareribs and prepare the coleslaw. A few hours before you plan to serve, prepare the squeezins, calabacitas and corn bread. Macerate the oranges. Serve buffet style outdoors.

INDIAN SUMMER PICNIC

For a fall foliage outing try packing this transportable menu.

icy cold beer and iced red zinger tea
Navajo Fry Bread *(p. 54)*
Tacos *(p. 92)*
mango and melon mélange with fresh lime

Prepare the fry bread shortly before leaving and pack in foil surrounded by several layers of newspaper. Prepare your favorite taco filling ingredients and place each in separate containers. Several hours or a day ahead of time combine slices of mango with melon balls, squeeze lime generously over the top and seal in a container. Chill the beer.

FIESTA

For fiestas of any size serve the following for a very traditional next-to-the-border feeling.

Margaritas *(p. 34)*
Guacamole *(p. 26)*
Tostados *(p. 32)*
Chile Pie *(p. 82)*
Empanaditas *(p. 30)*
Mexican beer
Chile con Queso *(p. 27)*

The day before the party or several days ahead, prepare the empanaditas and refrigerate or freeze. Prepare the tostados and the chile con queso the day before. A couple of hours or so before the party, chill the beer and squeeze lime juice around the Margarita glasses and salt the rims. If freezer space is available, chill the beer glasses. For the freshest flavor, guacamole must be made just seconds before serving.

COMIDA DE NAVIDAD
Christmas Eve or New Year's Eve Midnight Feast

A roaring fireplace and crisp mountain air make an ideal setting for this traditional dinner. If you serve this menu to start the New Year, fable has it that you will be blessed with prosperity. And who doesn't want that! I've traditionally served this menu throughout the years and especially liked it when I'm tucked away in a rustic setting with close friends. The foods are hearty, just right after an evening of toasting.

Mexican beer and champagne
Nachos *(p. 29)*
Tamales *(p. 104)*
Mexicali Salad *(p. 70)*
Wheat-Flour Tortillas *(p. 52)*
Flan Caramelisado *(p. 168)*
Mexican Coffee *(p. 40)*
Posole *(p. 113)*

Everything about this dinner is easily movable, making it especially suited for either packing and taking away or for preparing in advance for guests. The tamales, sauce, posole and tortillas can easily be prepared in advance and frozen if desired. Marinate the hearts of palm and olives a day ahead, then prepare the salad except for tossing a few hours ahead. The nacho ingredients can be laid out ready for last-minute combining and broiling. The flan can be made a few hours ahead.

MAIL ORDER SOURCES

Adobe House
127 Payne Street
Dallas, Texas 75207
(214) 748-0983

Alamo Tortilla Factory
329 St. John's Street
Titusville, Florida
(305) 267-7920

Ashley's, Inc.
6590 Montana Avenue
El Paso, Texas 79925
(915) 772-4217

Casa Moneo
210 West 14th Street
New York, New York 10011
(212) 929-1644

El Molino, Inc.
1078 Santa Fe Drive
Denver, Colorado 80204
(303) 623-7870

Frank Pizzini
202 Produce Row
San Antonio, Texas 78207
(512) 227-2082

La Semillera Horticultural Enterprises
P.O. Box 34082
Dallas, Texas 75234

Pecos River Spice Company
P.O. Box 680
New York, New York 10021
(212) 628-5374

Simon David Grocery Store
711 Inwood Road
Dallas, Texas 75209
(214) 352-1781

Stamoolis Brother's Grocery
2020 Penn Avenue
Pittsburgh, Pennsylvania 15222
(412) 471-7676

INDEX

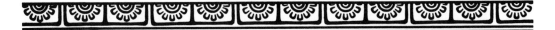